DOMINION IS OUR DESTINY.

We were born to be kings . . . but we live as slaves. We were born to rule, but we are imprisoned. How can we become what we were meant to be?

It is in Jesus that we see our destiny fully realized. THE SERVANT KING traces the life and lineage of the King of kings through the Book of Matthew, the first of the Gospels. "Take up your cross and follow Me," said Jesus to His followers.

If Jesus had come in glory first, we would have known His power . . . but not His love. God's love is not known in His glory, but in His brokenness; not in His throne, but in His Cross; not in might, but in servanthood.

As we walk in His Way, the power of the resurrection morning is promised to us now and forever.

LARRY RICHARDS
BIBLE ALIVE SERIES

The Servant King

The Life of Jesus on Earth
Studies in Matthew

David C. Cook Publishing Co.

ELGIN, ILLINOIS—WESTON, ONTARIO
LA HABRA, CALIFORNIA

SERVANT KING
Copyright © 1976 David C. Cook Publishing Co.
First Printing: November, 1976
Second Printing: January, 1978

Scripture quotations, unless otherwise noted, are from the New
International Version.

David C. Cook Publishing Co., Elgin, IL 60120

Printed in the United States of America

ISBN: 0-912692-99-5

Special acknowledgement is made for permission to quote from *New
Testament Survey* by Merrill C. Tenney, © 1961 Wm. B. Eerdman's
Publishing Co., and from *The Zondervan Pictorial Encyclopedia of the
Bible* edited by Merrill C. Tenney, © 1975 The Zondervan Corporation.

CONTENTS

THE SERVANT KING

THE SERVANT KING

TED DOESN'T THINK OF HIMSELF as a king. He's unhappy about his routine, low-paying job. He's uncertain about his future, hesitant to date, unwilling to assert himself. Life seems rather overwhelming to Ted, and he's terribly aware that he's being swept along without any sense of personal control.

Linda is a Christian, but frustrated right now. Her husband, really a nice guy and a nominal churchgoer when they married, is having a very difficult time in the stock brokerage business. He's deeply unhappy, plagued by doubts about his abilities and worth. Linda is frustrated for him and, because she wants him to become a believer so badly, she prays constantly, worrying about just the right words to say to bring him to God.

Linda doesn't think of herself as a queen.

It's strange. We can think of Jesus as King of kings—and miss the implication entirely. We can look at Jesus revealed in the New Testament as the Messiah, and not be aware that in His coming Jesus broke into history to free us to fulfill our destiny. Ted and Linda—and often you and I—miss out because we fail to grasp the full meaning of Jesus coming *for us.* For all the Teds and Lindas among us, Matthew's Gospel holds exciting hope.

GENEALOGY OF A MAN

Matthew 1:1-17

Genealogy is the first emphasis in the Gospel of Matthew. When we think of Jesus, we must realize that we are dealing with a man. The Person who came from Heaven (Jn. 1:1-2) is also fully human, and it is His heritage as a man that Matthew wants us to see.

Sometimes we hesitate here. Somehow, being a human being doesn't seem all that special. We picture man as a sinner, and recall the vast distortions that sin has swept into our individual and societal experience. We even find ourselves ashamed of our humanity at times. How far this attitude is from Scripture!

At the Creation, God made two striking affirmations. One, "Let us make man in our image, after our likeness" (Gen. 1:26a, KJV) tells us that our identity is not rooted in this world but in eternity. Only man, of all this creation, shares something of the likeness of God as a true person. The second, "Let them have dominion" (Gen. 1:26b, KJV) affirms that man was created to rule! We were born to be kings.

Even the entry of sin, while it warped our capacity to rule over creation and even over our own passions, did not change this destiny. The psalmist David caught a glimpse of our destiny, and in wonder penned Psalm 8:

When I look at thy heavens,
  the work of thy fingers,
the moon and the stars
  which thou hast established;
what is man that thou art mindful of him,
  and the son of man
    that thou dost care for him?

Yet thou hast made him little less than God,
  and dost crown him with glory and honor.
Thou hast given him dominion over
  the works of thy hands;
  thou hast put all things under his feet.
                                    Psalm 8:3-6, RSV

God created man—for dominion.

Probably the strongest emphasis on this truth is found in Hebrews 2, where the writer quoted Psalm 8 and noted, "In putting everything under him [man], God left nothing that is not subject to him. Yet at present," the writer went on, "we do not see everything subject to him. But we see Jesus, who was made a little lower than the angels, now crowned with glory and honor" (Heb. 2:8, 9).

In Jesus we see our destiny realized. He, the Man of Galilee, fulfilled the destiny of man by becoming

11

King, and in so doing was "bringing many sons to glory" (Heb. 2:10). Jesus was bringing you and me into our destiny—the experience of a dominion God has always intended for human beings to know! Jesus is King of kings, and we are the kings with whom and over whom He reigns.

Ted and Linda, and you and I, need not be overwhelmed by life. Through Jesus we enter into our unique destiny of dominion.

The Old Testament expectation. God's Old Testament people had dimly realized that dominion was their destiny. But they tended to think of dominion in a national sense, as that prophesied time when the nation Israel under the promised Jewish Messiah would be exalted over all the nations on earth. Their sense of destiny was accurate; God did make such promises. But their sense of destiny was limited; God intends far more through the ministry of the Messiah than Israel expected!

So it was very important that Matthew, who wrote primarily to the Jews, established the right of Jesus to the throne promised the Messiah. (The term "Messiah" in Hebrew means "the anointed one." It reflects the custom of anointing kings with oil when ordaining them in their royal office. You can see an illustration of this in Samuel's anointing of David as king of Israel, recorded in I Sam. 16.)

Two genealogical elements were critical if Matthew was to demonstrate Jesus' right to reign. The first was a relationship with Abraham (Mt. 1:1). It was from Abraham that Israel's awareness of her destiny sprang. God called this man from Ur

12

of the Chaldees and sent him to Palestine. There God gave Abraham great and special promises, promises that included possession of the land forever, a great people to live on it, a special relationship with God for Abraham's descendants, and ultimately a descendant (seed) through whom all the peoples of the earth would be blessed (see Gen. 12, 15, and 17). These promises, given in the form of a Covenant (a contract or oath), would be fulfilled through one man from Abraham's line.

The second significant genealogical element is relationship to David. Later in Israel's history God promised to David that the Messiah would come through his line. The ultimate King would be born from the family of David, Israel's greatest king. In tracing the genealogy of Jesus from Abraham and from David, Matthew was demonstrating Jesus' right to rule. Jesus' genealogy not only established His claim to be true man, but also His claim to the throne promised the seed.

In this genealogical record the focus of Matthew's Gospel becomes clear. We are invited in this book to see Jesus as King. Through Matthew's portrait of our Lord, you and I learn what dominion involves—and how to realize the destiny to which His Cross and Resurrection have lifted us today.

THE KING?

Matthew 1:18–2:23

One problem that Matthew faced in structuring his gospel for the Hebrew reader was to show that

Jesus really is the expected Messiah. Jesus didn't seem to be the King the Jews pictured. He did not crush the Roman Empire. He did not set up the expected earthly Kingdom. He did not act as they thought a king should act.

Theologically, then, Matthew had to answer several critical questions which the Jewish reader would naturally ask. Such questions as: "Is Jesus really the Messiah? Then why didn't He fulfill the prophecies about the Kingdom? What happened to the promised earthly Kingdom? If the Kingdom is not for now, then what is God's present purpose?" Very much aware of his reader's concerns, Matthew immediately tackled the first of these four critical questions.

One of Matthew's approaches to reach Hebrew readers was to use extensive quotes from the Old Testament. There are some 53 direct Old Testament quotes in Matthew, and some 76 allusions to the Old Testament, drawing from 25 of the 39 Old Testament books. Clearly Matthew was determined to bridge the gap between Old and New.

It's very significant to look at the contexts of the quotations used by Matthew in these first two chapters. Because of the Old Testament contexts to which Matthew linked Jesus, it is clear that He really is the expected King.

Micah 5:2 (Mt. 2:6) speaks of the Messiah as one whose origins are in eternity, who is to rule in Israel in the name of Jehovah, and who shall be great to the ends of the earth. In this man, Israel will find peace.

14

Jeremiah 23:5 (Mt. 2:2) pictures the Messiah as God and man. He is named "Jehovah our righteousness" (Jer. 23:6, ASV), and is born of David's line. He will reign over a people regathered after being scattered over the world. He will reign as King, and in His days Judah and Israel will dwell in safety.

Isaiah 11:1 (Mt. 2:23) stresses the Messiah's descent from the Davidic line. He will judge and rule with divine wisdom, and His rule will bring the destruction of the wicked. Gentiles as well as Jews will rally to Him, and in His day the earth is to be filled with a knowledge of the Lord. Even the realm of nature is to know unheard of peace.

The other references in these two chapters (no less than 16 all together) make it plain. Matthew was affirming that the Jesus he presented was the Messiah that Israel had been expecting. Jesus, the man who lived quietly, raised no army, taught, healed, and was dragged unprotesting to an agonizing execution, truly is the expected King of glory!

Later, the Jewish rabbis would try to explain the jolting contrast between the suffering Savior and the expected King by postulating two Messiahs: one, Messiah ben David who was yet to come and would rule; and two, Messiah ben Joseph, who perhaps had fulfilled the Old Testament prophecies associated with Messianic suffering. Who would have imagined before Jesus was born and lived His unique life that the pathway to glory led through suffering and self-emptying? Who would have dreamed that the concept of royalty and dominion contains an ingredient of brokenness? Certainly the Jews of Jesus' day, looking for the coming glory, did not see the majesty of suffering. And all too often you and I miss this dimension as well!

Matthew did not miss it. Matthew made it plain that the Jesus about whom he spoke to us *is* the King of glory. And with this fact firmly established, Matthew went on to describe a servant King, a King whose majesty is enhanced by suffering, a King who shows us the way to experience our own destiny of dominion—through a servanthood like His own.

TWO MODELS

Matthew 2

It's striking. Matthew no sooner introduces us to Jesus, Son of Abraham, Son of David, Israel's destined King, than he introduces us to another ruler. "After Jesus was born in Bethlehem in Judea, during the time of King Herod" (2:1). No two men could ever stand in starker contrast.

Herod. Herod the Great was the founder of a dynasty that plays a key role in Gospel history. We meet four generations of Herods in the New Testament. It is the founder (47-4 B.C.), aged and coming to the end of his life, whom we meet in Matthew 2.

Herod's father had attached himself to Julius Caesar's party, been made a Roman citizen, and

16

FIGURE I

THE HERODIAN FAMILY[1]

GENERATION I

HEROD THE GREAT
King of Judea
37-4 B.C.
Matthew 2:1-19
Luke 1:5

GENERATION II

Son of **Doris**
Antipater

Sons of **Mariamne**
Aristobulus
Alexander

Son of Mariamne of Simon
Herod Philip
4 B.C.-A.D. 34
(First husband of Herodias
—Matt. 14:3, Mark 6:17)

Sons of **Malthace**
*HEROD ANTIPAS
Tetrarch of Galilee
4 B.C.-A.D. 39
Luke 3:1, 19-20, Mark 6:14-29
Matt. 14:1-11
Luke 13:31 33, 23:7-12

*ARCHELAUS
Ethnarch of Judea
4 B.C.-A.D. 6
Matt. 2:22

Son of **Cleopatra**
*HEROD PHILIP
Tetrarch of Iturea
and Trachonitis
4 B.C.-A.D. 34
Luke 3:1

GENERATION III

*HEROD AGRIPPA I
King of Judea
A.D. 37-44
Acts 12:1-2—

Herod of Chalcis
A.D. 41-48

Herodias
Consort of Herod Antipas
Mark 6:17
Matt. 14:3

GENERATION IV

Bernice
became consort of her
brother
Acts 25:13

*HEROD AGRIPPA II
Tetrarch of Chalcis and
of northern territory
A.D. 50-70
Acts 25:13—26:32

Drusilla
married *FELIX
procurator of Judea
A.D. 52(?)-59(?)
Acts 24:24

Salome
Matt. 14:1-11
Mark 6:14-29

Reigning rulers of New Testament note are in capitals, wives
and relatives by marriage are in bold face. Other members
of the house designated by *

[1]The Zondervan Pictorial Encyclopedia o the Bible, Vol. II (Grand Rapids: Zondervan. 1975), p. 27.

17

appointed procurator (ruler) of Judea. Herod and his brothers were given government roles, but a decade of battling followed before Herod was proclaimed king of Judea by Rome and was able to enforce his rule. As king, Herod was both brutal and decisive, punishing or executing his enemies, and rewarding his friends. Rivals were murdered. When the decisive battle for the Roman Empire was fought between Anthony and Octavian (later to become "Augustus"), Herod gained the victor's friendship and was given control of additional lands.

While Herod's power was growing, his control over himself and his family was slipping. Herod had married 10 wives and had a number of sons. While these sons schemed to gain the throne, his wives hatched plots and counterplots. Herod became more and more suspicious and paranoid, even torturing his sons' friends to discover any plots against his own life. Herod's own character as a plotter who never hesitated to resort to murder was being reproduced in his family, and this led to the aging tyrant's own sense of terror and fear. Herod finally had the two sons of his favorite wife, Mariamne, executed by strangulation in the very city where he had married their mother 30 years earlier. Antipater, Herod's oldest son and designated heir, tried to poison his father and was put in chains.

When nearly 70 years old, Herod was stricken with an incurable disease.

It was at this time, shortly before his death, that

Herod heard of wise men who were seeking to worship the newborn King of the Jews. Herod summoned the wise men and made them promise to report the whereabouts of the child so he could "go and worship him" (Mt. 2:8,). The dying man still struggled to grasp the power that had brought him and his family only suspicion and hatred and death!

God warned the wise men to return home another way. And God warned Joseph to flee with the Christ Child to Egypt. Herod, realizing that the wise men had returned to the East without reporting to him, had all the male children of Bethlehem two years old and under killed.

It was then only a few days before Herod's death. Five days before Herod expired he had his son Antipater executed. Then he called all the leading Jews of his territory to the palace. When they came he imprisoned them, giving orders that they were all to be killed the moment he died, so there would be national mourning rather than rejoicing at his passing!

Herod's dream of power and glory had turned into a nightmare. The desperate king struggled to the last to maintain control over his kingdom, long after he had lost all control over himself. And so he died.

Jesus. As the hateful old man was living his last days in the splendor of a marble palace, a child was born in a stable. There, surrounded by the warmth of the animals which shared His birthplace, Jesus entered our world and became a part of a family so poor that Mary had to offer two doves rather than the prescribed lamb as the sacrifice for her purification.

The child would grow up in a small town far from the seat of power. He would become a carpenter, to live and labor in obscurity for 30 years. Finally, as a young man, the Carpenter from Nazareth would stand on a riverbank to be recognized by John the Baptist as the Son of God, destined to take away the sin of the world. For three years Jesus would walk the roads of Palestine, teaching and healing. He would raise no army. He would seek no earthly glory. He would ultimately humble Himself and accept death at the hands of selfish men who saw Him as a threat to their place and their power.

And through it all He would be a King.

A servant King.

A King in whom you and I find not only our redemption, but also find a pathway to the unique dominion over ourselves and our circumstances to which God has destined man.

THE CHOICE

In contrasting Herod and Jesus, Matthew implicitly presented his Jewish readers, and us, with a distinctive choice. We can continue to see *dominion* in terms of its outward glory and power, or we can look beyond the external to discover the inner core of greatness.

There was nothing wrong with the picture the

Jews had of the Messianic Kingdom. Later Matthew reported Jesus' own affirmation that that expression of the Kingdom would come. Even after the Resurrection the disciples themselves could not shake their longing for the coming glory. "Are you at this time going to restore the kingdom to Israel?" they asked. Gently Jesus responded, "It is not for you to know the times or dates" (Acts 1:6, 7). That Kingdom will come, in God's good time.

But until then Jesus remains King, and dominion is still ours in Him! If we can but shake the Herod dream and see in Jesus' humility the true key to greatness and glory, we can find a distinctive freedom that the world around us, stumbling over the external, can never understand. It is a journey toward just this kind of inner freedom that we're taking as we trace our Messiah's steps with Matthew.

For He *is* the King of kings.

In Him we grasp our title deed to rule.

GOING DEEPER

to personalize

1. Ted and Linda are real people who feel that their life is out of control. All of us have that feeling at times. Jot down areas in your life where you feel right now that you somehow lack dominion.

2. Read through the familiar chapters of Matthew 1 and 2, and then look carefully at the contexts of the Old Testament passages quoted there. Develop from these Old Testament locations

21

a careful portrait of King Jesus. The key references: Matthew 1:23 (Isa. 7:14); Matthew 2:2 (Jer. 23:5; Zech. 9:9); Matthew 2:6 (Mic. 5:2); Matthew 2:15 (Hos. 11:1; Ex. 4:22); Matthew 2:18 (Jer. 31:15); Matthew 2:23 (Isa. 11:1).

3. From the portrait given in the Old Testament passages above, *contrast* Jesus with Herod (text, pp. 16-19). From this contrast study, can you develop a tentative definition of "dominion"?

to probe

1. There are several issues which appear in these two chapters of Matthew that you may want to research in depth. Check them out in such resources as *The Zondervan Pictorial Encyclopedia of the Bible.*

(a) Who were the Magi (wise men)?

(b) Why does the genealogy of Matthew differ from that given in Luke?

(c) Examine in more detail the career of Herod the Great. What was he really like?

(d) What characteristics of Bible genealogies explain the artificial division of the line of Jesus into three groups of seven?

2. Trace the Bible's teaching concerning "dominion." Use a concordance to get at this theme, which is introduced in Genesis 1, and culminates in Revelation 22 with the promise that in eternity God's servants will see God's face and worship Him, and "they will reign for ever and ever."

Give as detailed an exposition as you can in two typewritten pages of what the Bible says about our destiny of dominion.

THE KING IS COMING

THE QUIET DRAMA of Jesus' birth in Bethlehem was the culmination of centuries of special preparation. The world into which Jesus was born had been uniquely designed. His birth was "when the time had fully come," Paul wrote in Galatians 4:4. All was ready.

ONE WORLD 350-4 B.C.

The world of Christ's day was unified in a way that our world had never been unified before. A common language provided channels by which the Gospel message would quickly spread. A single political power maintained a massive authority which wiped out old national boundaries and freed men to travel the known world. These unique conditions were vital in the later spread of the new faith.

Alexander. Alexander the Great had been responsible for the spreading of the overarching culture and language of this worldwide civilization. Alexander, a Macedonian, had set out over three centuries before Christ to conquer the world. His goal was to spread Greek culture, which he firmly believed was superior to all others. By 333 B.C. he had conquered the whole of Syria and Palestine; by 331 he had added Egypt. The whole vast Persian empire was his. But in 323, after touching India itself, Alexander died. His holdings were divided between four generals, and the unity Alexander envisioned was shattered.

In the East, Egypt and Palestine were held by Ptolemy and his descendents. Syria was ruled by the Seleucids. There was constant struggle between these two powers; finally in 198 B.C., Jerusalem and the Jews came under the sway of the Seleucids.

Rome. Following Alexander's day, the city on the Tiber River in Italy continued to expand its influence. Each new conquest led to further conquests as the Romans sought more distant borders to insulate their empire's heartland. Gradually the borders pushed outward to include what is now Spain, France, parts of Germany, part of Britain, and the Black Sea coasts of Asia Minor. Ultimately the Roman Empire extended from Spain to Armenia and from Britain to the Sahara.

By Jesus' day the whole Western world was knit together as Rome's empire: a single unit over which Rome maintained control. The language and culture were Greek (Hellenic). Alexander's dream had been realized through the agency of another race!

24

But Rome herself had not been stable. In the last ineffective days of the Republic, a form of government under which the Romans were supposedly ruled by a senate of many legislators, the central authority had broken down. In times of emergency, generals like Pompey and Julius Caesar, who won the loyalty of their armies, assumed the real power. After the assassination of Julius Caesar in 44 B.C., the empire drifted into a decade of civil wars. The decisive battle was fought at Actium in 31, and the victor, Octavian (Augustus) became Rome's "first citizen" and virtual dictator. Augustus, with his other gifts, was a brilliant administrator. He succeeded in bringing to the Roman Empire a period of unmatched stability and prosperity. Thus the world into which Jesus was born had known some twenty-five years of Roman peace (the *Pax Romana*)—a peace imposed by the power of Roman arms, and maintained by the administrative and political genius of the emperor.

THE DAYS OF THE HAMMER

Palestine: 198-4 B.C.

The ancient world was seldom a quiet one. Wars and rivalries troubled even the least significant backwaters. For decades wars had scarred Palestine and helped shape in Israel a special hunger for the promised Messianic King.

In the early division of Alexander's empire, as we have seen, Palestine fell to the Ptolemies. This

25

house seemed genuinely concerned about Alexander's dream. They developed the city of Alexandria, Egypt, as a center of culture and learning. The largest library in the world was established, and Jewish rabbis labored there to translate the Old Testament into the Greek language, a version known as the Septuagint.

But in 198 B.C. control of Palestine shifted to the Seleucids (Syria), who adopted an aggressive policy of Hellenization (imposing Greek culture, language, and religion). After a series of wars much like those through which Herod later would come to power, rule of the Seleucid empire passed to Antiochus IV Epiphanes. He determined to unify the diverse peoples under his control through Hellenization, and his program included religious unification around himself as *theos epiphanes,* the manifest god.

Antiochus set up his own high priest in Jerusalem, selling the office to the highest bidder, who plundered the Temple riches to pay off his bid. In the meantime, Antiochus defeated the Ptolemies, and even occupied Egypt. There Antiochus, at the head of his victorious army, was confronted by a representative of Rome who commanded Antiochus to vacate Egypt's rich land. Antiochus had spent 12 years as a hostage in Rome and knew Rome's power well. Cowed, he turned back. But he was furious now, and he determined to concentrate on making Palestine a buffer state between Syria and Egypt; and immediately he began a crash program to Hellenize the Jews.

Antiochus desecrated the Jerusalem Temple, offering on the altar a pig in sacrifice to Zeus, and he forbade practice of the Jewish religion. With one command, he sought to destroy the ancient Hebrew faith and life-style.

In Jerusalem many Hellenized Jews accepted Antiochus' commands. But not so in the villages. In the small village of Modein, a priest, Mattathias, was ordered to make a sacrifice to Antiochus. He refused. When another Jew volunteered to make the sacrifice, Mattathias killed the traitor and the Syrian legate, and fled into the Judean mountains with his five sons. This began the Maccabean rebellion in 166 B.C.

Mattathias died in 166 B.C. and leadership passed to his third son, Judas. Judas, nicknamed *Maccabaeus* ("hammerer"), led a growing revolt against the Seleucids. The dramatic exploits of the Maccabees, as they were popularly known, can be read in the books of I & II Maccabees. At one point Judas defeated an army sent by Antiochus. Soon the entire country was under Maccabean control!

But there were still inner struggles between bitterly divided Jews. After the death of Antiochus (163) and a defeat of the Jews by Lysias (the general over Palestine), Syria guaranteed the Jews religious freedom in 162 B.C. But Judas now insisted on political freedom as well, and the battle continued to 160. Judas appealed to Rome for protection, and his request was granted. But before Rome could step in, a swift Syrian attack led to a Jewish defeat and Judas' death.

Other sons of Mattathias took up the struggle, and a long line of Maccabean (Hasmonean) leaders resulted. Though internal rivalries plagued the land, Judea finally realized a degree of autonomy as the Seleucids gradually lost their power and authority.

But in 63 B.C. when two Hasmonean rulers contended for control of Judea, and both appealed to Pompey (the Roman general) for support, Palestine was firmly annexed as part of the Roman world, just as Syria had been in 65 B.C. Soon Egypt would also know Rome's sway (30 B.C.).

The Maccabees' vision of a free and independent Palestine had been buried by the inexorable march of history. But the dream had not been lost. Its roots were sunk deep in Old Testament prophecy and promise. One day God's Messiah would appear. And then—then the empire would be *theirs!*

So the land waited.

Augustus, good administrator that he was, ordered a census of the Roman world for tax purposes. In Palestine, Joseph went back to his home-town of Bethlehem to be enrolled. Mary went with him, even though it was nearly time for the birth of her first child.

Entering the city, the young woman reached out to clutch Joseph's arm. "It's time."

And it was time, the time that had "fully come" (Gal. 4:4).

All history had converged on this moment.

Augustus in Rome would never dream that God had guided him to power to bring world peace.

28

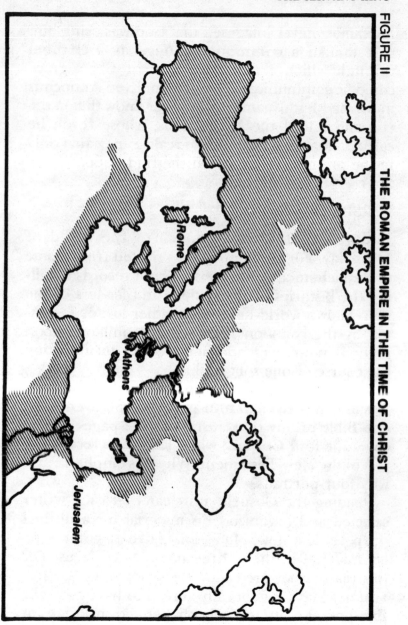

FIGURE II

THE ROMAN EMPIRE IN THE TIME OF CHRIST

Alexander never imagined that God was using him to establish a common language as a channel through which a new revelation of God's grace could be communicated to all men. Even Antiochus in his maddest dreams could never know that in the rise and fall of the Maccabeans, whose revolt he caused, Israel would be led to realize anew that only in the promised King could she find hope.

PERSPECTIVES

Today few of us know much of the world of Jesus' day. For us the focus has shifted from Rome to Bethlehem and Nazareth. Those records detailing the histories of the nations and leaders of the then known world have been either lost or forgotten by the common man; instead, millions upon millions pour over another record, documenting the course of one solitary life.

We ourselves fail to realize how much of our New Testament is given to four portraits of our Lord. In one Bible on my desk just now, 102 pages of text cover the four Gospels, while 134 pages record the rest of the New Testament. Why this emphasis, and why four portraits?

Reading the Gospels, it's clear that each writer selected and organized his material for a distinct purpose. Matthew, Mark, and Luke all cover similar material in their three portraits of Jesus. For this reason they are called the synoptic Gospels.

Mark. Mark is generally agreed to have been the first gospel written, probably penned in Rome for

Gentile believers. Jewish coloring is lacking, and where Palestinian customs are included, Mark explains them for a non-Jewish audience. The book is brief—a mere 661 verses, and seems to be a fast-moving, eyewitness account of Jesus' life, with great emphasis on the passion week and Christ's culminating act of redemption.

Both Matthew and Luke probably took Mark as a guide, in that they seemed to generally follow his chronology and sequence of events, although each made changes for emphasis.

Luke. Luke is the most comprehensive gospel, covering more of Christ's life than any other. Luke seemed particularly sensitive to Jesus' humanity, stressing His relationships with men in need, and including individuals left out of the other accounts. Luke mentioned 13 women not found elsewhere in the Gospels, and also included several case histories of men whose ways of life made them social outcasts, and who were transformed by Jesus' touch.

Luke's stated aim (Lk. 1:1-4) was to provide a clear, accurate historical account. He combined detail with a beautiful and sensitive portrait of the personality of Jesus, and of Jesus' love for all men.

Matthew. The first of the Gospels in our New Testament was probably written after Mark, and has a distinct and clear purpose. It was written to demonstrate to the Jew familiar with the Old Testament that Jesus is indeed the Messiah. Because of this emphasis, Matthew is the bridge between Old and New Testaments.

In addition, Matthew gives great prominence to

31

Jesus' teaching, with five blocks of teaching included which are absent from Mark.

Of the three, Matthew is the key gospel for us to explore. Its Old Testament context and flavor, and its purpose of bridging the Old Covenant and the New, make mastery of Matthew critical for the Bible student.

John. John's Gospel is distinctly different, and focuses on presenting Jesus as the Son of God. Where Mark and Luke launched the story of Jesus with His birth, John traced His origin back into eternity (Jn. 1).

In keeping with his purpose, John selected incidents and events that were different from those reported by the other three Evangelists. He reported different speeches, usually ones set in Judea. These are often long, theological and argumentative. Against the background of Judean unbelief, Jesus presented Himself as the bread of Heaven, the giver of life, the true light, and the ultimate truth.

John's Gospel is so significant that it is explored, along with Revelation, another writing of John, in the final book of this Bible Alive series, in which the Servant King is revealed as the Man of glory.

From the earliest days of the Church, Matthew, Mark, Luke, and John have been accepted as apostolic accounts of Jesus' life and ministry, and viewed as one collection. Through these ancient eyewitness accounts, we are uniquely introduced to Jesus.

Here we meet Him.

FIGURE III

JESUS' LIFE ON EARTH

Emphases	Birth	Victor	Moral Teacher	Miracle Worker	Controversialist	Leader	Prophet	Suffering Saviour
MATTHEW	1—3	4	5—7	8—9	10—17	17—20	13, 21—25	26—28
MARK				1—5	6—8	9—12	13	14—16
LUKE	1—3	4	6	5, 7—8	19—20	9—18	21	22—24

JOHN—emphases on **Controversialist, Leader,** and **Saviour** throughout

	Kingdom Emphasis	Turning Point	Cross Emphasis
MATTHEW	4—15	16	17—28
MARK	1—7	8	9—16
LUKE	4—9	9:22-27	10—24
JOHN	—	—	1—21

In these accounts of His words and actions, we realize that, as on this man all history seems to converge, so on Him must converge our faith and our lives as well.

We recognize Him as Israel's promised King.

We thrill to Him as our Redeemer.

And we puzzle over His words and ways, struggling to understand His servanthood, and find in His example the pathway to our own destiny as kings.

GOING DEEPER

to personalize

Look in a library to research all you can about one of the following:
1. Alexander the Great
2. Augustus Caesar
3. Antiochus (IV) Epiphanes
4. The Maccabees
5. Hellenistic culture
6. Pax Romana

to probe

1. Do you think it's accurate to see international and individual history today as God's work? Why or why not?

2. What can you see in your own life which might be viewed as God's preparation of you to become the person you are, or to do the work you're doing?

PREPARE THE WAY

IN A.D. 28 one of the Old Testament prophets returned. It had been nearly 400 years, and God had been silent. Malachi, the last of those Old Testament greats, closed his book with a promise—and a warning. "Behold, I will send you Elijah the prophet before the coming of the great and dreadful day of the Lord; and he shall turn the heart of the fathers to the children, and the heart of the children to their fathers, lest I come and smite the earth with a curse" (Mal. 4:5, 6, KJV).

Thus, the Jews had been guided to turn their eyes ahead, toward the time of the Messiah's coming. They were promised a forerunner, someone to warn them and turn their hearts back to God's ways. Implicit in Malachi's words was a choice. Unless the hearts of God's people were turned, the Messiah's coming would not bring Israel the expected blessing, but a curse.

Later Jesus would tell the crowds that John, then

executed by Herod (a son of Herod the Great), was the greatest of all the prophets and was, in fact, a messenger sent to prepare the Messiah's way. And Jesus added these strange words: "If you are willing to accept it, he is the Elijah who was to come" (Mt. 11:14). Israel did not accept John's Elijah-ministry. Their hearts would not turn. The golden opportunity slipped by. The Messiah's body came to fit a wooden cross rather than an ivory throne, and Israel was destined to know another 2,000 years of scattering, of ghettos, of pogroms, of un-realized hopes. History would now pivot to focus on the Second Coming of the Messiah. The fulfill-ment of Malachi's words would await another Elijah.

JOHN

Matthew 3:1-12

John's background. Luke 1 tells us about John's birth. He was born into a priestly family, his father, Zacharias, being one of the many politically unim-portant men who served the Temple two weeks ·a year and lived the rest of the time at his own farm in the countryside. Probably John was trained for the priestly ministry as well. The privilege was passed on from father to son, reserved by Old Tes-tament Law for the .descendants of Aaron.

Perhaps John, like Habakkuk, was shaken by the ritualism and emptiness of his day. We do know that from his birth John was filled with the Spirit.

John went to live in the wilderness. He ate wild honey and protein-rich locusts, and wore a scratchy shirt made of camel's hair. When the time was right, John began to preach beside the Jordan.

John's ministry. John's stern and bold words echoed the messages of earlier prophets. They, too, had condemned sin and called God's people back to the way of holiness outlined in the Old Testament Law. But there were differences.

The content of John's message was not really new. Luke 3:10-14 gives specific content; to each group or individual who begged guidance, John's prescription was a return to the righteousness and love expressed in the Law.

But several things about John's preaching were new: (1) John spoke with a peculiar urgency. "Hurry," he urged the crowds who came out to hear him or simply to gaze at the spectacle. "Repent, for the kingdom of heaven is near" (Mt. 3:2). John focused their attention not on the distant future of Israel but on their present situation.

(2) Another new focus in John's ministry was on the personal responsibility of the individual for himself. There had always been an element of personal responsibility in the prophetic messages. But now John warned against a hope anchored in some distant relationship to Abraham. "Do not think you can say to yourselves, 'We have Abraham as our father'" (Mt. 3:9), he cried, and then urged individuals to repent and to show by their changed lives an inner, personal commitment to God.

(3) John introduced baptism as a sign and sym-

bol of repentance. Baptism had been known in Judaism before. But John transformed baptism, giving it a fresh moral and eschatological significance. One who was baptized confessed his sins, identified himself with the renewal of the Kingdom under the coming Messiah, and committed himself to live a holy life.

There was another unique dimension to John's preaching: (4) John recognized himself as the promised forerunner sent to prepare the Messiah's way. Seven times the New Testament records John's announcement that the one to follow him was greater than he (Mt. 3:11; Mk. 1:7; Lk. 3:16; Jn. 1:25, 27, 30; Acts 13:25). The warning—and the invitation—were given. The crowds came and listened. Many were baptized. Many, particularly those of the religious elite who were quick to put themselves in the forefront of any popular movement, could see no harm in the rite, but they were withered by John's angry denunciation of them as a "brood of vipers" (3:7).

Soon everyone in the tiny land of Palestine had heard of God's firebrand in the desert. They gossiped excitedly about whether he might be the Messiah, and they waited to see what would come next.

JESUS' BAPTISM

Matthew 3:13-17

"Then Jesus came from Galilee to the Jordan to be baptized by John" (3:13).

38

Here a fascinating confrontation took place. John objected! It would be more appropriate for Jesus to baptize John; John was sure that Jesus did not need his repentance-oriented rite.

It's tempting here to think that John recognized Jesus as the Messiah. But the Bible tells us that the day after the baptism John pointed Jesus out as the Messiah to two of his followers: "I would not have known him, except that the one who sent me to baptize with water told me, 'The man on whom you see the Spirit come down and remain is he who will baptize with the Holy Spirit' " (Jn. 1:33). All the four Gospels agree that John saw the Holy Spirit in dove form descend on Jesus after He went up from the water after baptism. Clearly John did not object to Jesus' baptism on the grounds of His Messiahship.

The mystery may be resolved when we realize that John and Jesus were cousins. Their mothers were very close (cf. Lk. 1:36-45). Probably the two young men, both now about 30, had spent much time together, meeting each year with their families at the three annual feasts in Jerusalem when all males over 12 were to appear, and exchanging visits during the rest of the year as relatives do everywhere. John's objection to baptizing Jesus may have been based on a simple fact: John knew that Jesus had no need to repent. John knew that Jesus' life was in fullest harmony with the laws and ways of God—in fuller harmony than even his own!

Jesus overcame John's objection. It's only right, He pointed out, to identify yourself with right things (3:15). Entering the water with John, Jesus was baptized, thus identifying Himself fully with John's message as well as with the men and women who flocked to receive that baptism because of their own deep need.

The baptism of Jesus launched His public ministry. But it did even more than that. It demonstrated how fully Christ as a man identified Himself with humanity. One of the central doctrines of the Christian faith is that of the *Incarnation*. Isaiah had foretold it: "A virgin shall conceive, and bear a son and shall call his name Immanuel" (Isa. 7:14, ASV). The name, giving it the emphasis of its Hebrew form, means *"With us* is God!" God, in the person of the child of promise, would fully identify Himself as a human. In every way this promised individual would be God with us.

Both Matthew and Luke report the birth of Jesus and explain how Mary, before her marriage with Joseph was consummated, miraculously conceived through the direct intervention of God. The child was in a totally unique sense the Son of God—God Himself come to enter the race of man in the only way in which He could become truly human. Jesus is fully identified with us in our humanity. He is God. And He is man.

Hebrews 2 points out that it was fitting for Jesus to be like us in every way, including subjection to human weaknesses, and susceptibility to suffering. "Since the children have flesh and blood," the writer explains, "he [Jesus] too shared in their humanity (2:14). Dying, Jesus could then deliver us from

40

our lifelong slavery. God's concern for man drove Jesus to "be made like his brothers in every way" (2:17) and, becoming a faithful high priest, He offered Himself as the expiation for our sins. The writer to the Hebrews concludes, "Because he himself has suffered when he was tempted, he is able to help those who are being tempted" (2:18).

The full humanity of Jesus is a basic teaching of our Bible. It was necessary for Jesus to be truly human for Him to become our sacrifice. It was necessary for Jesus to be truly human for Him not only to free us from lifelong bondage, but also to aid us in our own temptations and sufferings.

No wonder John, meeting his cousin Jesus on the Jordan riverbank, protested against baptizing Him—he recognized Jesus as a good and righteous man. Jesus Christ, as a man, was so fully identified with man that even those most impressed with His spiritual qualities never dreamed that He was the Son of God!

There's a lesson here for each of us. What do we look for when we're seeking evidence of God's work in our life or in another's? Some startling, miraculous sign? Something that sets the person apart from all other men? Or are we looking for a work of God within: a work of God that produces the love, joy, peace, patience, kindness, goodness, faithfulness, gentleness, and self-control which God values so highly (Gal. 5:22, 23)? Are we looking for a person who is different, or for a person who demonstrates the very best of what humanity can be? How strikingly our Lord's experience with

41

John points it out. The spiritual person is, in fact, the most humane and human of us all.

Once the voice of God had spoken from heaven, "This is my Son, whom I love; with him I am well-pleased" (Mt. 3:17), John realized the obvious.

Of course Jesus was the Messiah!

Of course this most perfect man had to be the promised redeemer. The virgin had brought forth a Son, a Son who was the "with us" God. God had identified Himself in every way with the humanity He came to free and to lift to share His throne.

THE TEMPTATION

Matthew 4:1-11

If the baptism of Jesus impresses us with the complete identification of the Savior with us in our humanity, His temptation stretches our minds to grasp the depths to which He had stooped.

In theology, Jesus' self-humbling is called the *kenosis:* the emptying. Paul develops it briefly in Philippians 2, speaking there of Jesus, "who, being in very nature God, did not consider equality with God something to be grasped, but made himself nothing, taking the very nature of a servant, being made in human likeness. And being found in appearance as a man, he humbled himself and became obedient to death—even death on a cross!" (vss. 6-8). Simply stated, the Bible affirms that when Jesus entered our world He set aside the power and privileges of deity. He consciously limited Himself to live as a man. Even the miracles Jesus would later perform would be attributed by Him to the power of the Spirit (Mk. 3:22-30). The emptying process Paul describes is one of progressive humiliation. Jesus . . .

- emptied Himself
- was born in man's likeness
- was obedient even when it meant death
- accepted even the shameful death of an outcast criminal

THE KING CHOSE TO BE BROKEN

When we read about the temptation of Christ in Matthew 4, we have to read the story against the background of the kenosis. When a physically weakened Jesus, after forty days of fasting in the desert, was tempted by Satan, He did not seek strength from His divine nature to resist. The very first words of Jesus in response to Satan's initial temptation set the tone.

"If you are the Son of God," Satan challenged, "tell these stones to become bread." Jesus answered with a quote from Deuteronomy: "Man does not live by bread alone, but on every word that comes from the mouth of God" (Mt. 4:2-4).

See it? *"Man* does not live by bread alone!"

Addressed as the Son of God, Jesus affirmed His intention to live on our earth as a man. Subject, as you and I are, to the hungers and drives and needs which throb within and seek to pull us into sin, Jesus met Satan's temptations. He would continue

43

to meet each earthly trial in all the vulnerability and weakness that are ours. Rejecting the privilege that was His by virtue of His deity, Jesus cast His lot totally with you and me.

Because of this great act of self-emptying, you and I can find hope. For Jesus overcame temptation—as a human! Committing Himself to be responsive to God and God's Word, Jesus showed us the possibility and the pathway to dominion.

There are three temptations recorded in Matthew, as there are in Luke. But the order differs between these two Gospels. Each writer reported the experience of Jesus with a view to highlighting the culminating test from his own perspective.

Luke, whose focus is on Jesus as a warm and real human being, saw the temptation to throw Himself down from the Temple's pinnacle and prove that the Father was with Him as the culminating test. Each of us has times when we feel deserted by God, when things have gone wrong and we doubt His continued concern for us. As the Old Testament passages quoted stress, the issue in this temptation was that of putting God to just such a test, to see "is the Lord among us, or not?" (Ex. 17:7, KJV).

But Matthew saw this temptation as less significant for Jesus than the vision Satan spread before Him of all the kingdoms of the world. "These can be yours," the tempter enticed, "if only you will worship me." The man born to be King was shown the kingdoms that would be His, and was reminded

44

that they could become His now. All the suffering could be avoided—all the anguish, all the rejection, all the intimate pain of a death in which the weight of the world's sin would bear down on the sinless one.

And again Jesus chose. "It is written: 'Worship the Lord your God, and serve him only' " (Mt. 4:10). Complete commitment to the will of God was Jesus' pathway to the throne. There could be no shortcuts. There could be no other way.

Before Jesus could rule, He had to learn by experience the fullest meaning of submission to the Father's will. The crown lay beyond the Cross.

THE KING'S WAY

After the testing was past, Matthew includes a brief sketch of Jesus as He launched His public ministry. Jesus took up John's theme and preached that the Kingdom was near at hand (Mt. 4:17). He chose disciples (4:18-22). He went about Galilee teaching in the synagogues and healing (4:23, 24). Soon the crowds that followed John swirled around Him (4:25).

But it is only the briefest sketch. In these chapters, Matthew only mentions the public ministry. All the hurry, all the excitement, and all the converging of the crowds to see the miracles and hear this man who spoke of God with such authority, seem unimportant compared to two initial portraits of the King. First there is the picture of Jesus submitting to John's baptism, identifying Himself fully

45

with man. And then comes the picture of an emptied Jesus—suffering, tested, opening Himself to the full force of temptation in His vulnerability as a human.

What is the meaning of this emphasis for us? We see at least four lessons immediately brought home.

(1) Jesus truly was determined to be a servant king. The Incarnation does not mean that Jesus had stopped being God, but that He had freely set aside His rights as deity. The outward exercise of power and glory was not essential to His majesty. In choosing to empty and to humble Himself, Jesus displayed God's highway to dominion.

When Cathy met Earl and fell in love with him, she determined to become the center of his world. Gradually, she shut out his old friends. After they were engaged she became even more adept in manipulating him to keep him to herself. Cathy took Herod's route in search of power. Manipulating, selfish, she was always trying to control.

Cathy wants to fill the throne of Earl's life. She wants to be queen, but a commanding and not a servant queen.

How different with Jesus. Whatever dominion may involve, and whatever it means for us to reign, our destiny is not to be found in selfishness, but in self-emptying.

(2) Jesus' full identification with us in our humanity gives hope. If Jesus had overcome the tempter in His nature *as God,* we could hardly expect to overcome. We're not divine. But Jesus met Satan as a *human.* So we can dare to believe that our

dominion destiny includes the power to overcome!

Ted, the young man we met in chapter 1, views life hopelessly. He feels caught, trapped, overwhelmed by a life that is out of control. Seeing Jesus become vulnerable and yet become the victor can change Ted's whole perspective—and ours. Hebrews says it: "Because he himself suffered when he was tempted, he is able to help those who are being tempted" (2:18). In Jesus, the human, you and I find help—and hope.

(3) Jesus' response to the tempter spotlights resources that you and I can draw on to overcome. In each case, Jesus went back to the Word of God and found a principle by which He chose to live.

This is important. It is not simply "the Word" that is our resource. It is the commitment to live by the Word. It is resting the full weight of our confidence on what God says, and choosing in each situation to do that which is in harmony with His revealed will.

This resource which Jesus used to overcome is our resource too. But we must use Scripture in Jesus' way.

(4) Jesus is portrayed in Matthew 3 and 4 as a person in full control—of Himself! In fact, we might even view this as the central message of these chapters. Jesus demonstrates His right to reign by proving that He has authority over the worst of man's enemies—himself.

Certainly Israel had known in Herod a king who had absolute power over others, but he was powerless to control his own hatreds and his fears. Since

47

then, in our Napoleons and Hitlers and Stalins, we've seen over and over again that enslaving others brings the ruler no freedom within.

Yet it is exactly here that our dominion rule as kings under the King of kings must begin. We must gain power over ourselves: power to humble ourselves, power to submit to God, power to give up our rights, power to obey. The outward glory and the pomp of worldly power are nothing compared to this authority over what is within.

Jesus demonstrated just this kind of authority.

In His humility, Jesus was exalted above the greatest men our world has ever known. Jesus alone fully controlled the world within.

No wonder Matthew wants us to know this truth: Jesus has overcome! He and He alone is worthy to be proclaimed King.

GOING DEEPER

to personalize

1. Read Matthew 3, 4 and Luke 4.

2. There have been several theories presented about Jesus' baptism. How would you evaluate each, and why?

   (a) Jesus was seeking forgiveness.
   (b) Jesus was dedicating Himself to His mission.
   (c) Jesus was entering into the priestly office.
   (d) Jesus at this point became God's Son when the Spirit anointed Him.
   (e) Jesus was identifying Himself with John's message and movement.

48

3. Do a careful in-depth study of the three temptations. Through what avenue of human vulnerability was each attack launched? (For instance, the challenge to make bread was an attack focused on Jesus' physical needs and sensations.) What principle did Jesus use against each attack? How many normal temptations that you are subject to can you jot down for each of the three avenues of vulnerability? How would you apply the principle Jesus used in each of these temptations? What choices would each principle suggest you make in the given situations?

4. Look at the four "lessons" suggested by the author on pages 46, 47. Which of these is most important to you personally, and why?

to probe

1. Examine in theology books the doctrine of Jesus' two natures, focusing on the meaning of His being a true human. Also explore carefully the doctrine of the kenosis. Summarize your findings in a three-page paper.

2. Develop a sermon or Bible study based on Jesus' temptation. How would you structure it to help the learners realize the practical impact of this passage on their own personal lives? Hand in a detailed outline of your approach and methods.

49

"THY KINGDOM COME"

MATTHEW TELLS US that, after His baptism, "Jesus began to preach, 'Repent, for the kingdom of heaven is near' " (4:17). Book after book has been written exploring Jesus' Kingdom emphasis, puzzling over the exact thrust of His words.

God as King over all. All agree that the Bible pictures God as King over His creation. In this sense God is sovereign, marking out the course of cultures and the process of the ages. In a universal sense, everything and all times are to be viewed as God's Kingdom: a realm over which He exercises control.

It is also true that the Old Testament brings a special focus to God's kingly rule. God in a special way rules over Israel; He is Israel's true King (Deut. 33:5; I Sam. 12:12), and Israel is His kingdom (I Chr. 17:14; 28:5). In a distinctive sense, God involved Himself in the control and direction of Israel's destiny.

When we read in the New Testament that Christ is "head over everything for the church, which is his body" (Eph. 1:22, 23), we have a parallel to the Old Testament emphasis. The rule of God extends over all—but finds special focus in His concern for His own.

God's future reign. A reading of the Old Testament makes it plain that there is more involved in talk of a kingdom than God's overarching rule. God promised through the prophets that a day would come when He would set up an everlasting Kingdom on earth and personally rule from Zion (Isa. 24:23; Mic. 4:6, 7; Zech. 14:9-17, etc.). Daniel and Isaiah add their descriptions: the King will be God, and yet of David's line. When the Messiah comes, the rule of God will find visible and overwhelming expression as God openly exercises His once hidden power.

It is this Kingdom the Jews expected and yearned for. It is this Kingdom which is described in the prophecies which Matthew relates to Jesus.

So we can hardly doubt what His hearers pictured in their minds when Jesus proclaimed the good news that the Kingdom was at hand. His listeners were sure He meant the eschatological expression of the rule of God. They thought "Kingdom of Heaven" must mean God's revelation of His power and goodness through the Messiah's righteous, endless reign.

Near? It is here that many hesitate. Jesus said that the Kingdom of Heaven was "near." Yet, 2,000 years have fled since that announcement, and the visible earthly Kingdom His hearers expected has not come. So some have stepped back and denied the Old Testament vision. They have tried to make the "Kingdom of Heaven" simply another affirmation that God is in charge after all.

But why then did Jesus say that the Kingdom was finally "near"? Why the urgency? Why, if God has *always* maintained that kind of rule? Clearly some other aspect of the Kingdom than God's universal rule must be drawing near.

Particularly significant is the Greek word translated "near." It can mean "at hand" or "has arrived." Was Jesus' announcement of the Kingdom an affirmation that in His own coming God's kingly action was already breaking in uniquely on time and space?

Usually we think of "kingdom" as a place. The "kingdom of Lichtenstein" is geographically defined: a tiny bit of land. Certainly the Old Testament picture of God's ultimate Kingdom does involve a place: Palestine is the center from which the Messiah will rule, and the whole earth will be His Kingdom's limitless extent. However, in rabbinic literature, the kingdom emphasis is not on a *place* but on *action!* "The kingdom of heaven" speaks of that divine action which breaks into our universe and marks out events as God's accomplishment.

No wonder Jesus taught the disciples to pray and to say,

> Your kingdom come,
> Your will be done
> On earth as it is in heaven.
>
> *Matthew 6:10*

53

Jesus' disciples, then and now, are to look to God to act on earth just as He acts in Heaven itself to bring His will to pass.

It is most likely, then, that Jesus' announcement of the Kingdom had a dual emphasis. On the one hand, Jesus was announcing the nearness of the promised eschatological Kingdom in which God will act visibly and dramatically to enforce His will. Israel was offered the future Kingdom for which they longed in the person of the King.

On the other hand, Jesus was also announcing that the Kingdom had arrived! In the presence of the King, God had taken a personal hand in human affairs. In Jesus Christ, God was already bringing His final gift of deliverance and dominion to men.

THE SERMON ON THE MOUNT

Matthew 5:1-11

This impact of the Kingdom message does not strike us with the same force that it would have struck the believer of Jesus' day. We have the entire New Testament revelation; we're aware that Jesus acts today in our lives through the Holy Spirit.

But to the men and women who heard Jesus teach, this Kingdom concept was new and powerful. They were used to looking ahead to a future when God would act. Jesus' Kingdom message made them realize that God was already exercising kingly authority. We can expect God to act *now* to work out His will in you and me!

54

This Kingdom emphasis on an active God underlies what we today call the Sermon on the Mount. Only those who throw the full weight of their confidence on God as a King who acts in and for them *now* can ever locate the courage to live the startling life-style which Jesus laid out for His disciples (Mt. 5:1).

Interpreting the sermon. There have been various approaches to interpreting the Sermon on the Mount. Some are clearly designed to explain away our need to take its teachings seriously.

(1) One view sees this sermon as a salvation message for the world. By "being good" an individual can live in harmony with God and earn His approval.

Only a person who is blind to his own sin and who ignores Jesus' command to repent can see the sermon as portraying a way to find God.

(2) Another view insists that Matthew 5 contains "kingdom truth." The ways of living portrayed are the ways men will live when Jesus reigns, but they aren't practical for us till then. Too often this approach, which has a certain validity, is used to excuse behavior and attitudes that fall far short of the standard Jesus expressed here.

(3) A third view suggests that the sermon is addressed primarily to the Church. This, too, has some validity, but it overlooks the fact that at this stage in Jesus' ministry, Israel, and not the Church, was central.

(4) A fourth view synthesizes and provides a better balance. First, the sermon is to be seen as a

detailed exposition for Jesus' hearers of what repentance (which literally means a "change of direction" or "about face") involves. Second, it does picture life in the eschatological Kingdom. When God is in full charge of the end of time, everyone *will* live by these guidelines. Third, we have in the Sermon on the Mount the most detailed exposition of God's ethical standards given in the Word. Because these standards reflect God's character and reveal His will, they are relevant to us today as well as in the future Kingdom.

(5) To these traditional interpretations, we need to add a fifth. The Sermon on the Mount describes the way in which men are freed to live when they commit themselves to the kingship of God. When men of any age realize that *in Jesus* the Kingdom is "near" for them, they are free to abandon themselves totally to God's will, confident that, as they obey, He will act to shape events.

THE KINGDOM NOW

When Wayne Adams began to dream of making available high-quality art with a subtle yet powerful Christian message, the vision seemed impossible. Wayne had no background or contacts in the art world. And he had no money to finance such a ministry.

But Wayne began to pray. Within weeks, believers with all the needed skills were located. Wayne also prayed for funds and left his well-paying job to concentrate on the dream. He sold his car to get enough money for a start; insurance from a burglary of his home met other needs. By December 1974, 2,000 prints of the first painting, *Born Again,* were completed.

Today Christian bookstores throughout the country carry Witness Art paintings, and many Christian homes, including my own, feature these lovely testimonies to some of the great realities of our faith.

Looked at from a sensible point of view, everything Wayne did to launch this ministry was foolishness. He left his job. He entered a field in which he was less than a novice. He sold his car when the money ran out, and used insurance funds to pay the bills for his new project rather than refurnish his home. Everything Wayne did *was* foolish— unless God's Kingdom has broken into our world and unless God Himself acts in our lives to accomplish His will. Given the reality of God's rule, a person like Wayne, who sets the Lord on the throne of his own life, is not foolish but wise.

The Bible makes it clear just how wise Wayne was. According to Colossians, God in Christ "has rescued us from the dominion of darkness and brought us into the kingdom of the Son he loves" (1:13). The Christian has been torn from Satan's grasp and planted firmly in a relationship with God in which Christ is King—a relationship in which Christ acts in our lives.

The Sermon on the Mount is for men who have chosen to be Jesus' disciples and have freely submitted themselves to the King (Mt. 5:1). In it Jesus

57

explains to His disciples of every age what living as a citizen of Heaven's Kingdom involves. As it meant for Wayne, living in the Kingdom means, for us, abandoning the ways of the world to adopt a diametrically different set of values and commitments.

New values (Mt. 5:1-12). When first heard by disciples, the familiar words of the Beatitudes must have sounded jolting and strange. Familiarity has made them palatable today; their stark challenge to our deepest notions about life is easily passed over. But that first time the challenge must have been almost overwhelming.

What Jesus did in these few verses was to set up a new system of values by which His people are to live. Implicit is a rejection of the values which lie at the core of human civilizations and which shape most individual personalities.

It's difficult to live in our world, to look at men and women who live by the values in the column on the right, and be unaffected. We admire the popular, successful, and self-reliant businessman. We envy his power and his ability to indulge in the good things this world has to offer. It's only natural to want to be like him; we appreciate the values on which his life has been built.

We also admire this world's "beautiful people." Their sophistication, looks, pleasures, and importance draw us. We appreciate the values which their lives express. That whole attractive package of values is appealing to us because we tend to associate them with fulfillment. To be and behave like the

FIGURE IV **THE BEATITUDES Matthew 5:3-10**

Jesus' Value	Countervalues
BLESSED ARE THOSE WHO ...	**BLESSED ARE THOSE WHO ARE ...**
(vs. 3) are poor in spirit	self-confident competent self-reliant
(vs. 4) mourn	pleasure-seeking hedonistic "the beautiful people"
(vs. 5) are meek	proud powerful important
(vs. 6) hunger for righteousness	satisfied "well adjusted" practical
(vs. 7) are merciful	self-righteous "able to take care of themselves"
(vs. 8) are pure in heart	"adult" sophisticated broad-minded
(vs. 9) are peacemakers	competitive aggressive
(vs. 10) are persecuted because of righteousness	adaptable popular "don't rock the boat"

people who have status in our society becomes our dream.

Jesus shatters such dreams and rejects such goals in the Beatitudes. He sets up a whole new package

59

of values, proclaiming that in *these* you and I will find fulfillment. Not in pleasure, but in longing. Not in satisfaction, but in hunger. Not in popularity, but in commitment to an unpopular cause. Not in competition and "winning," but in helping others win their way to peace.

The First Beatitude illustrates them all. "Blessed are the poor in spirit," Jesus says. Blessed are those who do not approach life with confidence in themselves or reliance on their gifts or talents, sure that they are competent to meet life's challenges. Blessed are those who approach life *without* such self-based confidence, "for theirs is the kingdom of heaven." *Not,* theirs "will be" the Kingdom of Heaven. But, theirs *is* the Kingdom of Heaven. In approaching life humbly and with full reliance on the King, we open up our lives to His direction. We open up our present and future to Jesus' kingly action.

Commitment to Kingdom values brings us to the place where we ask the King to reign in our lives. When Wayne Adams surrendered his competencies to God and launched Witness Art, depending on God to shape events, Wayne responded to the leading of the King and committed himself to the values of the Kingdom. In becoming one of the poor in Spirit, Wayne discovered the reality of Jesus' promise: "Theirs *is* the kingdom of heaven."

New behaviors (Mt. 5:13-16). Values are always expressed in action. What is truly important to us finds its way into our daily lives.

This is what Jesus alludes to in two brief word

pictures. Those who hold Kingdom values will witness to those around them of the reality of the Kingdom. "You are the salt of the earth," Jesus said. In Palestine, flakes of salt form on the rock shore of the Dead Sea at night. In the morning the sun rises. Under its heat the salt loses its saltiness. It blends with the shore and loses its distinctiveness.

"You are the light of the earth," Jesus went on. Lamps are designed to be put up on a lampstand in full view, not to be hidden.

Both these word pictures help us realize that the values which we hold as citizens of Jesus' Kingdom are to find expression in our behavior, so that our difference from men of the world might be made plain. Those who come to know us will gradually realize that we are different because of our relationship with our Father "in heaven" (vs. 16). The Kingdom of Heaven is to break into the world, today, through you and me.

Case histories (Mt. 5:17-42). Jesus' Kingdom teaching focused first on values and on the behaviors through which values are expressed. The Lord now goes on to give a number of illustrations. This "case history" approach is in full harmony with Old Testament practice. After the Ten Commandments are recorded in Exodus 20, the next few chapters similarly illustrate the principles with examples.

Jesus begins (5:17-20) by explaining that His teaching is not contrary to Old Testament Law, but goes beyond it. Unlike the Law which was unable to produce righteousness, the Kingdom life-style fulfills the Law's requirements by producing a righ-

61

teousness that "surpasses that of the Pharisees and the teachers of the law" (5:20).

Each of the following cases demonstrates how the Law is "fulfilled." In each, the focus shifts from behavior (which the Law regulated) to intent and motive. The King works in the hearts of men, changing the values and motives from which behavior springs. In the Kingdom, outward conformity without inward commitment will never do!

Murder? Jesus locates the first step in anger and hatred (Mt. 5:21-26). Rather than nursing anger, which may lead to murder, the Kingdom citizen is to value peacemaking. He is to take the initiative to be reconciled to his brother. Later John would write, "Anyone who hates his brother is a murderer" (I Jn. 3:15).

Adultery? The "fulfilled" Law is not just concerned with the act, but with lust itself (Mt. 5:27-30). Jesus sarcastically suggested to men quick to excuse themselves by claims that "I saw her, and couldn't help myself," that they try to rid themselves of their problem by plucking out the offending eye! Impossible? Surely, and so again the issue is focused on the place where the problem lies: "in the heart."

Divorce? Moses permitted it, but Jesus calls for lifelong commitment (Mt. 5:31-32).

Promises? Make your word binding by signing contracts—and feel free to break a promise sealed with a handshake (Mt. 5:33-37)? No, be the kind of person whose yes always means yes, and whose no means no.

62

What about revenge and repaying those who harm you (Mt. 5:38-48)? The Law says you can insist on your rights and on repayment. But in the Kingdom, God's blessing rests on the merciful. In relationships with people now, the Kingdom citizen is called on to be like the Father in Heaven and to love even enemies. Does this deny justice? Not at all! It recognizes the fact that in the Kingdom, *God* is the One who acts. Paul later put it in these words: "Do not take revenge, my friends, but leave room for God's wrath; for it is written: 'It is mine to avenge, I will repay, says the Lord" (Rom. 12:19). Abandoning the values and the instincts which lie at the root of man's society, the Kingdom citizen is to build his life on those peculiar values Jesus taught, values that seem all too shabby to most people. Poverty of spirit? Mourning, meekness, hunger for righteousness? Mercy, purity, peacemaking, willingness to be persecuted on God's account? Yes. Upon these values Jesus invites His hearers to build a new life.

THE RISK

There are two things that are immediately striking about this part of Jesus' Sermon on the Mount. First of all, a person who takes the call seriously and attempts to live as a Kingdom citizen takes a great risk. Each of the countervalues of the world seems to have great survival value! If you aren't competitive and aggressive, you'll never get ahead! If you can't take the practical course and make the expedient choice, you're just asking for trouble.

Jesus' sermon calls men to abandon this whole approach to life and to walk out of step with society. Like Wayne Adams, we are called to abandon "wisdom" for responsiveness to God's will—whatever the apparent cost. And this involves a risk.

The second thing we see in the sermon is the impossibility of the standards Jesus maintains. In shifting attention from behavior to values and motives, Jesus sets righteousness even farther from us than it was before. You and I may have been relatively successful in controlling our behavior, but what about our desires? Our thought life? Our emotions and feelings toward others? If righteousness in the Kingdom means purity in the inner man, each of us is helpless!

But this is just the point of Jesus' announcement. The Kingdom is "at hand"! In Jesus Christ, God has begun to take that action which culminates in our total freedom. In the ultimate expression of the Kingdom, Jesus will reign over a renewed earth. But even before Jesus returns, believers of every age have been "brought" by God to the "kingdom of the Son he loves" (Col. 1:13). You and I are in a relationship with God in which He acts for us. When we grasp this, when we open up our lives to Jesus' royal control, He will break into the pattern of our daily lives and into the very heart of our character. Owning Jesus as King, we turn our fears over to Him and seek to rebuild our lives on that which He values.

Jesus is King. We can afford the risk.

GOING DEEPER

to personalize

1. Read Matthew 5 through several times, jotting down questions you may have.

2. Look at the chart on page 59. What additional "countervalues" can you suggest which are in contrast to the values Jesus suggests in each Beatitude?

3. Why not take *one* of the Beatitudes, trace the meaning of the word and its use in Scripture, and write a one-page paper on the life-style this word suggests—and the life-style it rejects.

4. Read each of the short "cases" following the Beatitudes, and relate each case to one of the values they suggest. Two cases in the text have already been so related (see pp. 60, 62).

to probe

1. Read at least one commentary or short book on the Sermon on the Mount.

2. Research the "Kingdom of Heaven" in at least two books. How do the authors understand it? Summarize their views in writing, comparing them with the view of the author in this text.

SEARCH FOR THE KINGDOM

JESUS' LISTENERS WERE HUNGRY for the Kingdom. His message was a jolting one, yet many followed and listened eagerly. They sensed that this Man, who taught with authority, had to know the way to the experience for which they yearned.

That hunger, that longing, is something you and I can understand. We've yearned for a fuller experience of God. We, too, have been looking for the Kingdom where Jesus reigns and acts. All too often we've missed it. All too often we've concluded that the Kingdom is wholly future, only to be known when Jesus comes again.

Part of the reason why we tend to look at the Kingdom as only future is that we've missed the Kingdom when we've looked back into history. Our view of history is distorted, a caricature that has little resemblance to reality. Usually the caricature is drawn something like this: "Everything was great as long as the apostles lived. Then it got bad, with the Church hardening into a dead and restricting institution paganized by Rome. Then Luther and Calvin brought the Protestant Reformation, and it was alive again for a while. But soon that drifted into deadness as well. Today we're just holding on (sometimes with a feeble grip!), waiting till Jesus comes."

This portrait of Church history is faulty. It comes in part from the tendency of historians to focus on the institutions, the popes, the cathedrals, and the books written by establishment men to sum up the wisdom of their age. But neither Thomas Aquinas' *Summa* nor John Calvin's *Institutes* expresses the Kingdom! The Kingdom is expressed in the living witness to Jesus which the Holy Spirit has burned into the lives of those whose hearts turn to the Lord.

For example, in the 12th century, the Waldensians, the Poor Men of Lyons, appeared. They gave the Bible to the people in the common language, stressed repentance and conversion, and also emphasized the living of a Christian life guided by all of Scripture, but especially the Sermon on the Mount.

Long before Luther, John Huss led a great revival in Prague, a revival later forced underground by the persecution which led to Huss' death. For 300 years an underground church existed in Bohemia, with the Gospel passed quietly from father to son, from grandparent to grandchild. Finally, these people found refuge in Germany on the estate of Count Nicholas Ludwig von Zinzendorf. Now called Moravians, they provided impetus for a great missionary movement leading to revivals in Germany, Holland, the Scandinavian countries, France, Switzerland and America, as well as England. It was Moravian missionaries who met John Wesley while on a ship going to America and introduced him to the possibility of personal faith in Jesus Christ. So, many years before Luther, small prayer and Bible-study groups dotted Germany; when God called Luther to the Reformation leadership, followers had already been prepared.

Today the United States sends out thousands of missionaries across the world. But as late as 1800, there was no missionary movement to reach abroad. Then in 1806, college students at Williams College in Massachusetts began to discuss their part in sharing the Gospel with the non-Christian world. A sudden rainstorm sent them dashing into a haystack. Praying there together, God called the first American missionaries. Adoniram Judson, Luther Rice, and Samuel Mills were to lead a host of young men and women crossing the oceans to take the Gospel to the world.

These illustrations, which can be multiplied to touch every century and every nation where the Gospel has taken root, bear a striking similarity. They began in quiet, hidden ways. As far as what has become known as "Church history," they often stand outside of the great monuments and acts which men tend to record! The haystack, and not the cathedral, is often the characteristic of the Kingdom.

True, these movements have often forced their way into the history books. A city set on a hill cannot be hid; a light placed on a candlestick cannot be ignored. But all too often, whether the movement has been in Catholicism or Protestantism, the historical record is of persecution and antagonism and fear. As in Jesus' day, institutions tend to teach the traditions of men rather than those of God, and such institutions are threatened by the Kingdom.

The Kingdom comes into conflict with the world, even as Jesus ultimately was forced into open conflict with the religious men who demanded with insistent shouts, "Crucify Him!"

WHERE THE KINGDOM IS NOT

Matthew 6:1–7:23

It would be wrong to conclude from what I've just shared that the Kingdom is always in contrast with the established or the institutional church. The Wesleyan revival led to the formation of the Methodist churches. The touch of the Kingdom was not removed as soon as this church institutionalized. Today there are Methodist churches which are living expressions of the Kingdom—and Methodist churches which are dead and know no touch of Kingdom life.

The point made by Church history is that institutions can never be *identified* with the Kingdom. The Kingdom can sweep into man's edifices—and sweep out again. To perceive the Kingdom, we must look beyond the outward appearances to the fleshed-out life of Christ in His Body.

This is hard for seekers to grasp. You and I, who are looking for the Kingdom of Jesus and eager for Him to reign and act in our lives, often become confused. We look to the wrong things for light to guide us. It is exactly this tendency to miss the inner reality of the Kingdom in the outward trappings of religion which Jesus deals with in this next section of the Sermon on the Mount. In Matthew 6 and 7, He gives us four warnings—warnings against plausible pathways which will inexorably lead us further and further away from the Kingdom's presence in our daily lives.

Visible piety (Mt. 6:1-17). "Be careful," Jesus says, "not to do your 'acts of righteousness' before men, to be seen by them" (6:1).

It's a very natural thing to want to be appreciated as men and women of God and looked to with respect. It's healthy to want to be a leader. But there are many religious games played by men and women of every age which draw them away from the Kingdom.

In Jesus' day, one game was to have a trumpeter announce it when someone was going to give alms to the poor. The poor would come—and so would a host of admiring observers. Everyone would watch as the giver earned a reputation for piety and generosity.

Another common game was played with prayer. When a man wanted to pray he would go to a busy street corner or a well-filled synagogue and stand to pray aloud. Often he would pray prolonged and wordy prayers, giving evidence to all that he was pious. Even when men took a vow to go without food, they would be sure to look pained and would rub dirt onto their faces so all could see how much they were suffering for God!

These games were played not for God but for other men, to be seen by them and to win a reputation for piety.

Tragically, many in Jesus' day thought that these men truly were pious. They felt that the way to find the Kingdom was through imitating their public acts of piety. An earnest seeker could be drawn into a life-style that was hypocritical: "play acting."

In contrast, three times in these passages, Jesus instructs us, "But when you give to the needy, do not let your left hand know what your right hand is doing, so that your giving may be *in secret*. Then your Father, who sees what is done *in secret*, will reward you" (6:3, 4). And when we pray, "Go into your room . . . and pray to your Father, who is unseen. Then your Father, who sees what is done *in secret*, will reward you" (6:6). Fasting, too, is to be seen only by "your Father, who is unseen; and your Father, who sees what is done *in secret*, will reward you" (6:18).

It is tremendously important for us to grasp the impact of the repeated emphasis. Kingdom reality can not be measured by the external things which, done to be seen by men, are singled out in each age as evidence of spirituality.

In one of the churches I attended as a young

Christian there were a number of external measurements: attendance at the meetings of the church, praying in King James words at prayer meetings, teaching in the Sunday school, carrying tracts to hand out at the subway station, refraining from smoking and drinking and movies—and from close association with anyone who did indulge in the forbidden three. Most men and women in our little church conformed to these externals. Yet, I know now that beneath the surface of public piety many suffered the emptiness and pain of alienation and were unfulfilled. I know also that when I struggled to find reality through conforming, I, too, wandered away from the reality.

What then is the alternate road? If we are to look away from the ways our culture measures public piety, to what do we look? Jesus' answer is that we are to look to an "in secret" relationship with God as our Father. We are to cultivate awareness that He is present, and are to act to please the One who sees us in secret.

This picture of God seeing us reflects an Old Testament notion of God's concern for His children. Peter quotes a psalm that says it well: "For the eyes of the Lord are on the righteous, and his ears are attentive to their prayer" (I Pet. 3:12). The apostle is pointing out in this passage that the God who sees, orders events. Even when suffering enters our life, that, too, is a beneficient expression of God's active will (I Pet. 3:13-17). When we act in full awareness that we are in the presence of the Father, He sees, and He rewards.

73

How significant then is the four times repeated "in secret"? The world around us does not see the Father. Even our brothers and sisters may see no visible sign of God's presence. In this age, before Jesus comes in power, the Kingdom and the Father exist "in secret." But the God who sees us in secret does reward us. The God who sees us is, and He acts in the world of here and now!

If we seek the Kingdom, we dare not let the traditions of the men of our age draw our attention away from the God who *is*. It is our secret life with Him which is the key to our Kingdom experience.

Material success (Mt. 6:19-33). Jesus' second warning focuses on possessions. In His day, even the disciples believed that wealth was a sign of God's blessing. Thus, the rich man was viewed as being close to God, while the poor man was somehow thought of as being under His judgment. Jesus put material possessions in a totally different frame of reference in this passage of the sermon.

"Do not store up for yourselves treasures on earth" (6:19). Instead, treasures are to be laid up in heaven. Once again we are confronted by the fact that the Kingdom in our day is in secret. It cannot be measured by any material achievement.

But Jesus went beyond warning against such a measurement of the Kingdom. He said, "Do not" lay up such treasures. Jesus explained why by pointing out that a concentration on material success would lead to the darkened eye and the divided heart. The eye is the organ of perception through which our whole personality is guided

74

(6:22, 23). If we focus our vision on what the world calls success, our perception will be distorted and the light of God's revelation of reality blocked out. Our whole personality will be darkened.

What's more, our will is affected as well. God and "success" will compete in our personality, and our values will be shaped by a commitment to one or to the other. "You cannot serve God and Money" (6:24).

Then Jesus went beyond, to lay bare the basic issue. Jesus tells us we are not even to be anxious about our life! We reject the laying up of earthly treasures, and we reject concern about what we eat and drink (6:31). Living in the Kingdom means abandoning our very life to the Father's care so that we can concentrate on seeking "first his kingdom and his righteousness" (6:33).

How can we find the courage to abandon our lives to God's care? Jesus' illustration answers us. God feeds the birds and clothes the flowers—and you and I are of infinitely more value to our Father! His power orders every detail of the world in which we live; knowing His power and knowing His love for us, His children, we abandon ourselves to His loving care, knowing that He will meet our needs.

Authority (7:1-13). "Do not judge" are the warning words which mark off the third section of Jesus' guidelines for Kingdom seekers. It is directed at those who see in the Kingdom the right to exalt themselves above their fellow citizens, who are named "brothers" here.

The first warning dealt with seeking approval of others rather than God.

The second warning dealt with having concern for this world rather than abandoning such concern to seek the Kingdom and righteousness.

The third warning dealt with relationships within the Kingdom.

This warning is a vital one; in human society we always go about establishing a "pecking order." We try to quickly settle the question of who has control over another. The whole "chain of command" approach of the military or the business world or any other human institution reflects the concern men feel for authority. The right to judge another is a right which the human heart yearns for.

This is as true in the Church as in any group of men and women. Church history is in a real sense a report of the struggle for control over others in the name of religion. This is not true only in the papal distortions of the Middle Ages. It is true in the local Protestant church of today where a pastor or a board member may struggle to impose his will on his brothers and sisters. Or where a gossip may claim the right to exalt herself or himself over the person whose reputation is smeared. Pushing others down is one way we try to exalt ourselves.

But if we are to find the Kingdom, we have to abandon all claims of a right to judge. "Do not judge," Jesus says, and for all time He destroys the pretentions of anyone who would seek to exalt himself over others in the Kingdom (7:1-6).

Instead Jesus teaches us the right attitude: the

attitude of humility and servanthood. "Ask," Jesus teaches, commanding us to take the position not of a judge but of a supplicant. We are to approach life in the Kingdom with a deep sense of our own need for God's good gifts—and with full confidence that our loving Father will supply us with all we need (7:7-11). What is more, in bowing down to God we also bow down to our brothers. We commit ourselves not to judge them but to serve them: "In everything do to others what you would have them do to you" (7:12).

This truly is a narrow gate. But it leads us to life—the life of the Kingdom, now (7:13-14).

False leaders (7:15-23). Jesus concluded His warnings by focusing on men who will claim Jesus as Lord, but who will seek to use and savage His flock. How will the false prophet be known? Not by what he says so much as by what he is and does. "By their fruits you will recognize them" is how Jesus put it (7:20). In context, the bitter fruits are obvious.

Men will come claiming Jesus as Lord and offering to lead the way into the Kingdom. But their lives will be marked by a public rather than a private kind of piety, by a concern for rather than an abandoning of material things, and by a claim of authority to judge their brothers and sisters in the Kingdom.

When these marks are seen, we have Jesus' declaration that, no matter what mighty works they accomplish in His name (7:22), "I never knew you" (7:23). Such men cannot lead us into an experience of the Kingdom.

THE KINGDOM FOUND

Matthew 7:24-27

Jesus' message concluded with a simple yet powerful illustration that focuses our attention on the one road to experience of the Kingdom now.

> Therefore, everyone who hears these words of mine and puts them into practice is like a wise man who built his house on the rock. The rain came down, the streams rose, and the winds blew and beat against that house; yet it did not fall, because it had its foundation on the rock. But everyone who hears these words of mine and does not put them into practice is like a foolish man who built his house on sand. The rain came down, the streams rose, and the winds blew and beat against that house, and it fell with a great crash.

We stand at a fork in a road that leads only two ways—Jesus' way, or another. We, too, have heard the words of the King. We see the pathway He set out as leading to the Kingdom.

In Matthew 5, we heard Jesus focus the issue on our inner lives, and we explored the values on which we are called to build our lives. In Matthew 6 and 7, we spelled out specifically key values to reject and countervalues to accept. We must be impressed that the life-style Jesus presented is one of brokenness and abandonment.

We abandon the approval of men to care only for

the approval of God. We abandon concern for even the necessities of life to concentrate our attention on righteousness. We humble ourselves before our brothers, rejecting any claim of a right to judge them, and we take our place with them as supplicants before God. In our humility we put others' good first, and choose to serve.

Of course we'll find the Kingdom!

We will be following in the footsteps of the King.

GOING DEEPER

to personalize

1. Do you feel that you have ever really experienced the Kingdom? How? What would you expect experience of the Kingdom to involve?

2. What is the purpose or significance of the Lord's prayer which is included in this context (Mt. 6:9-13)? How does understanding the context make it even more significant as a pattern for us?

3. What kind of "piety games" do believers play today? Describe at least three of these games that are common now (cf. text pp. 72, 73).

4. How does Matthew 7:24-27 apply to you?

to probe

1. What is the relationship between the Kingdom and human institutions?

2. Apply your definition. What are its implications for *one* Christian organization of which you are a member?

79

SON OF MAN

THE LIVE TV STUDIO AUDIENCE broke into laughter each time one of the "Good Times" cast asked the pastor a question. His answer was always the same: a decisive "Perhaps."

It's funny on TV. But not in real life. Kay found that out as she went the round of her Christian friends, asking their advice and counsel. Some said one thing. Some another. No one seemed to be too sure. The uncertainty and conflicting ideas were confusing rather than helping her.

No wonder the crowds who listened to Jesus' Sermon on the Mount were stunned. No, not so much by what He said. That hadn't really sunk in yet. The words of the sermon would have to be remembered and thought about deeply before the new way of life Jesus sketched could become clear. What the crowds who heard Jesus were astonished at was His tone of *authority*. They were "amazed at his teaching, because he taught as one who had authority, not as their teachers of law" (7:28, 29). Christ claimed the King's right to govern His people; He spoke with authority. Now all would ask, did He truly have the authority He claimed?

AUTHENTICATION

Matthew 8:1–9:32

The next events seem to merge in a fast-paced narrative. Actions of the King are traced as over and over they demonstrate the validity of Jesus' claim of authority.

Willing and able (Mt. 8:1-13). Immediately upon Jesus' descent from the mountain on which He had spoken, a leper met Him. He said, "Lord, if you are willing, you can make me clean" (8:2). This man sensed Jesus' power but was uncertain if He would choose to use it for his sake. Jesus reached out and touched the leper, healing him. The King is willing to exercise His authority for man.

Entering the city of Capernaum, a Roman officer met Jesus to ask for the healing of a servant. Christ offered to go with the Roman, who objected, "I do not deserve to have you come under my roof" (8:8). Instead the Roman asked Jesus merely to speak the word. Jesus spoke; the servant was healed. Jesus is able.

Power over all (Mt. 8:14–9:31). The next event shows Jesus' authority over *all* the powers to which you and I are subject.

82

Sickness	Jesus heals.	8:14-17
Nature	Jesus stills the storm.	8:23-27
Demons	Jesus casts them out.	8:28-31
Sin	Jesus forgives.	9:1-8
Death	Jesus makes alive.	9:18-26

There is nothing to limit the authority of Jesus, who has demonstrated His power over everything under which you and I are crushed! This man *is* able to speak "as one having authority" (Mt. 7:29, KJV)—because He does.

INSIGHTS

There are three very special riches for us in this passage.

(1) *Under authority.* The Roman soldier speaking to Jesus said, "I myself am a man under authority, with soldiers under me. I tell this one, 'Go,' and he goes" (8:9). He said this to explain the confidence in Jesus which enabled him to ask Jesus to heal, from a distance, by the mere speaking of a word. His point was this: As a soldier, his authority over others was a *derived* authority. It was his relationship in the chain of command which gave this military man his power. When he spoke, all the power of Rome's mighty empire, under whose authority he stood, spoke through him.

And what about Jesus? Why was He able to speak and have nature, demons, and even death jump to obey? Because Jesus also operated under authority, the very authority of God. When Jesus spoke, all the limitless power of God Himself spoke through Him.

It's like this today. We can trust Jesus. The full power of Almighty God is His.

(2) *New wineskins.* A fascinating dialogue is inserted in Matthew 9:14-17. John the Baptist's disciples have noted that Jesus is unlike their master. They come to ask why. Jesus explains, and adds, "Neither do men pour new wine into old wineskins. If they do, the skins will burst, the wine will run out and the wineskins will be ruined. No, they pour new wine into new wineskins" (9:17).

You and I cannot stuff Jesus or our experience with Him into our old ways of thinking and living. Life with Jesus is a new and exciting thing. He Himself wants to fill us, to expand our personalities, and to reshape us to fit who He is. When Jesus, the Man with all power, comes into our lives, we are privileged to open ourselves up to newness!

(3) *Dead and blind.* Through these two chapters the acts of Jesus follow a progression. Each portrait shows Him as having power over a greater enemy than the last: sickness, nature, demons, sin, and then death itself.

Why then does an instance of healing the *blind* follow the raising of the ruler's daughter? For our sakes! You and I can find the faith to believe that Jesus will make us fully alive when He returns. But how often we look at the dead dimensions of our present life with despair. The blind men were living—but with dead eyes. When they begged for healing, Jesus asked, "Do you believe that I am able

84

to do this?" (9:28). They did believe. Jesus touched their eyes. And where the moment before there had been death, there was now sight.

Jesus comes into our lives with hope *for today*. If your personality has died to the capacity to live or shriveled in bitterness, or if you have lost the capacity for compassion, Jesus asks, "Do you believe that I am able?" We can answer, "Yes." Jesus has the power to bring life to the dead areas of our lives, now!

"THE SON OF MAN"

Matthew 8:1–9:32

To really understand the significance of the extended passage we've just been considering, we need to note one of its peculiarities. Throughout this sequence of events Jesus refers to Himself as "the Son of Man." He does not use the term in the Sermon on the Mount. The first occurrences are here.

The term "Son of Man" is found in both the Old and New Testaments. In the New it is used 94 times, and, with five exceptions, always by Christ Himself. Clearly Jesus is saying something important about Himself in His selection and use of this term.

On the one hand, of course, the phrase "Son of Man" emphasizes Jesus' full humanity. But even greater significance is found in the fact that, as in Matthew 9:6, it signifies Jesus' redemptive and au-

85

thoritative mission. In the term "Son of Man" Jesus presents Himself to us as the Victor.

God became man in order to bring other men into that Kingdom where His power can be exercised *for* us.

The demons recognized and spoke to Jesus as the "Son of God" (Mt. 8:29). They were right; they knew Him for who He is. The whole Bible makes it very clear that the One who became man at Bethlehem truly is the Creator God. John insists that Jesus is God, co-existing with the Father from the beginning (Jn. 1). Jesus does not hesitate to claim equality with God (Jn. 17). Paul's writings affirm Him as God, along with the Father and the Holy Spirit. The Old Testament speaks of Jesus in prophecy as the "father of eternity" (a phrase meaning the source or originator of eternity itself) and speaks of a child being born as "a son . . . given" (Isa. 9:6, KJV). The name Immanuel, as we have seen, means "With us is God." Jesus had every right to speak of Himself as the Son of God, for that is who He is.

But He chose for Himself the title "Son of Man." A man, with God's prerogative of forgiving sin. A man, with power to give life and to heal. A man, the Victor over death. In Jesus the very power of God entered the mainstream of human experience, and in Jesus' authority as the Son of Man you and I find a resting place for hope. Years ago Johann Burger (1598-1662) caught a vision of the authority of the Son of Man, and expressed it in the hymn, "Jesus Lives, and So Shall I."

Jesus lives and reigns supreme;
And His kingdom still remaining.
I shall also be with Him,
Ever living, ever reigning.
God has promised: be it must;
Jesus is my hope and trust.

The man with all power lives today. His Kingdom does remain. With Him, we shall reign also. Then, and now.

SHARED AUTHORITY

Matthew 9:35–10:40

Jesus' authority had been established. Then He did an amazing thing. "He called his twelve disciples to him *and gave them authority*" (10:1).

Immediately after establishing His own authority, you and I are taught that Jesus intended to share that authority with His followers.

It is human need that moved Jesus to this unexpected decision. Matthew 9:35-38 pictures Jesus continuing His itinerant mission, teaching and healing. Everywhere there were crowds; everywhere He saw men and women who were "harassed and helpless, like sheep without a shepherd" (9:36). Moved, He turned to His disciples. "Ask the Lord of the harvest, therefore, to send out workers into his harvest field" (9:38). Jesus determined to multiply His ministry by sending His disciples to every place where He Himself wanted to go.

It must have seemed exciting to His disciples. To be men, themselves harassed and helpless a short time before, but suddenly to have power! "Heal the sick," Jesus told them, "raise the dead, cleanse those who have leprosy, drive out demons" (10:8). With it all, they were to share the good news that the long-awaited Kingdom was at hand. But the thrill and pride must have been dampened as Jesus went on to explain the life-style of men who are given the gift of power.

They were not to go in pomp or luxury. They were to live among their fellowmen as Jesus did—humbly, as servants. And while Jesus' disciples were given authority over sickness, death and demonic powers (10:8), they were not to coerce men. Some people would receive them; some would hate them. The disciples role is to use authority to serve.

Life-style then. This chapter gives us deep insight into discipleship and helps us see ourselves as Kingdom citizens who have power—but humble ourselves to serve. Note these features of Jesus' instructions:

- Disciples are to be dependent on God, not on their own wealth or possessions, for necessities (10:8-11).
- Disciples are to give all men the freedom to accept or reject them and their Lord (10:12-15).
- Disciples are to expect and to endure persecution from those who reject and hate their Lord (10:16-25).
- Disciples are to remember their great value to

88

God the Father, and do His will without fear of men (10:26-33).

● Disciples are to expect conflict, even in their own homes. In everything, Jesus is to be put first, and pain is to be borne just as Jesus bore the pain of His Cross (10:34-39).

● Disciples can know they bring great gifts to men, who will be rewarded for their response to the Father and His children (10:40-42).

How very different from the life we expect of a man with power! Instead of wealth, there is self-chosen poverty and dependence. Instead of demanding power over others, all men are given freedom to choose. Instead of honor and praise, there are persecution and maligning. Jesus chose to empty Himself to win us victory as the Son of Man. So, too, disciples are called to wear the humble garb of servants as the badge of their authority.

When Jesus shares with us, He shares *all* that He is. We must always remember that He came as a *servant* King.

Life-style now. When I came home this past week from a school for pastors which I dean annually at Wheaton College's Graduate School the last week in July, my wife, Marla, and I sat up and talked until 3:00 a.m. In the week I'd been away she'd had an exciting time preparing for a small-group Bible study we attend. And she'd had several opportunities to minister to two of the young people in our neighborhood.

She knew the Lord had been with her in these

89

one-to-one experiences, but she was still feeling deep discouragement. We've known the young people for nearly two years; many hours have been given to talking with them and praying for them. Yet one boy remains unresponsive—listening, but choosing over and over again to go his own way. Last week he once again chose to steal, and was caught by the police.

Marla's feelings were so mixed. She has deeply cared for this young boy, yet over and over she has been hurt by his unresponsiveness and deceit. How could she keep on loving? How much she yearned simply to forget him, to put him out of her thoughts and heart. Yet, she couldn't. The pain of his rejection—of both of us and of the Lord—was overwhelming.

Together we looked at this very passage of Scripture and read words that Jesus spoke to His first disciples. "A student is not above his teacher, nor a servant above his master. It is enough for the student to be like his teacher, and the servant like his master" (Mt. 10:24). We talked of how Jesus felt rejected and vilified by the very people He became a Man to save. Jesus' power, used so freely for others, was not used for self-protection. He exposed Himself to hurt, "made himself nothing, taking the very nature of a servant" (Phil. 2:7).

So it must be for us as well. In Jesus, under His authority, we too reign. But like Him, we are servant kings.

With us Jesus has shared His authority, and His servanthood.

SHATTERED EXPECTATIONS

Matthew 11

Like chapter 10, Matthew 11 is completely discourse. While Matthew 10 is addressed to the disciples, chapter 11 is addressed to the crowds—crowds who, struggle as they will, cannot see a servant as their coming King.

The dialogue was initiated by disciples who had come from John the Baptist. The great prophet and forerunner of Jesus was in prison. Soon he would be executed by Herod, his head a prize won by the sensuous dance of a girl with whose mother Herod was living in sin. John had recognized Jesus at His baptism when the Lord was clearly marked out for him by God. But now, even John was wondering.

Why? Because John, too, expected the King and Kingdom to burst on Israel with outward power. Not even John had expected the coming of a servant King!

Jesus' answer was to direct John's disciples' attention to the acts of mercy He was performing. "Go back and report to John what you hear and see: The blind receive sight, the lame walk, those who have leprosy are cured, the deaf hear, the dead are raised, and the good news ispreached to the poor" (11:4, 5). John would grasp the meaning. John, like Jesus, was steeped in the lore of the Old Testament. His thoughts would turn to Isaiah 35 and he would remember the prophet's words about the glory and the majesty of God (35:2).

91

Behold, your God
　　will come with vengeance;
　　The recompense of God will come,
　　　But He will save you.
Then the eyes of the blind will be opened,
　　and the ears of the deaf will be unstopped.
Then the lame will leap like a deer,
　　and the tongue of the dumb will shout for
　　　joy.

Isaiah 35:4-6 (NASB)

John envisioned the glory primarily as recompense, as the day of God's judgment. But the glory of God was also seen in the tender care of the Messiah for men and women in need. John did not understand then that the servant ministry of Christ had to come first. But the report reassured him. Jesus *was* doing what the Scriptures foretold that the Messiah would do.

The crowds were not so easily satisfied. Jesus reminded them of John, and said that should they accept it, "He is the Elijah who was to come" (11:14). Clearly Jesus claimed to be the Messiah whom John announced (11:7-15).

But the people of Israel were unable to make up their minds. They were repelled by John's austerity and demand for repentance—he took his religion a little too seriously. And they were tempted to dismiss Jesus because, in contrast to John, He lived a normal life and was "a friend of tax collectors and 'sinners'" (11:19). Like people today, they wanted to have a God who fit *their* expectations. Yet, like changeable children, they couldn't make up their minds what He should be like. Each time a candidate appeared, they changed the rules (11:16-19).

Then Jesus uttered His first recorded words of warning and of judgment. He returned to the cities where His miracles had been done, and spoke sternly of coming woe. Even pagan Tyre and Sidon, even licentious Sodom, would have repented and believed if a messenger from God had come with such powerful authenticating works. But Israel still hesitated. Israel still refused to commit herself to her King (11:20-24).

The chapter closes with a prayer—and with an invitation. Israel's rejection of the King is also part of the Father's "gracious will." The nation might refuse its King, but all who labor and are heavy laden are called to come to the Savior. "Come to me," Jesus invites, "and I will give you rest. Take my yoke upon you and learn from me, for I am gentle and humble in heart, and you will find rest for your souls. For my yoke is easy and my burden is light" (11:28-30).

The word picture is a beautiful one. The yoke of Jesus' day was a fitted collar-like frame, shaped to rest on the neck and shoulders of two animals. Teamed together, the task was far easier for two oxen than for one. And if one were a young ox, how much easier to have an older, stronger companion to share the burden. To men who called for God's King to reign over them, Jesus offered to be God's servant, yoked in harness with them. Today, taking up the yoke that links us to Jesus, we too find rest. We walk beside Him. We learn from Him. And because our older, stronger, all-powerful Companion takes His fullest share of all our burdens, when we are linked to Jesus, you and I can find rest.

GOING DEEPER

to personalize

1. Read Matthew 8:1—9:31. Which of these evidences of Jesus' authority has the most relevance to you now? And why?

2. From Matthew 10, discover as many characteristics of *discipleship* as you can. Write these out.

3. From the above, select at least three characteristics, and from your own experience attempt to illustrate what they mean for believers today (the experiences can be either "successes" or involve analyses of "failures."

4. Write out what you thought the Christian life was like shortly after you became a believer. How do you see it now?

to probe

Look up every occurrence of the word "disciple" in the Book of Matthew. From your study:

1. Define what a disciple *is.*

2. Describe what a disciple *does.*

3. Explain how a disciple is *trained.*

94

HARDENING OPPOSITION

LAST NIGHT I LISTENED to a late night talk show on
which two well-known radio personalities were talking about visits each had made to the South American land of the Aucas. These were the jungle
peoples who in the late '50s speared five
missionaries—some of whose wives and children
later went to live among them and won them to
Christ. One of the radio personalities told how impressed he had been with the translated testimony
of a converted chief who had earlier taken 35
human heads, and by the fact that the actual killers
of the five had not only become Christians but were
now themselves missionaries to other jungle tribes.

Both men were tremendously impressed by their
trips and these jungle peoples. Their interest and
curiosity had been challenged—but not their commitment. Faced with the necessity of making a personal choice, neither had responded, and one was
clearly hostile.

It must have been something like this in Jesus' day. When He first came on the scene, teaching and healing, many were drawn to Him. He was a curiosity, someone to be impressed with and to talk about. Even the leaders of the people viewed Him as God's messenger (Jn. 3:2). But as Jesus' message became more clear, and as He confronted each hearer with the challenge to *choose,* attitudes began to change. His Sermon on the Mount spoke of the Kingdom in unexpected ways. His own behavior did not fit their idea of the coming King. His authenticating miracles could not be denied, but as His continued teaching more and more clearly exposed the fallacy of their own attitudes and ways, they became more hostile. Jesus was no longer a curiosity; He was a threat, demanding that they choose between His revelation of God and His ways, and their own dearly held beliefs.

Jesus' authority had clearly been demonstrated in His miracles; He exercises authority over *all* powers that hold men in bondage. It was clear that no Pharisee or Sadducee had similar power or authority. Yet their resistance grew. They would not believe.

In the men of Jesus' day we see a contemporary issue drawn as well. Rejection of Christ is seldom an issue which hangs on lack of knowledge. Rather, as issues are more and more clearly drawn, our response to truth hinges on our will. We must *choose.* For the non-Christian it becomes a choice to abandon hope in oneself and trust Jesus alone to bring a person into a family relationship with God. For the

Christian there is also a choice—a choice to follow the servant King and to adopt the life-style of the Kingdom, or to hold onto the attitudes and values and beliefs and behaviors of the world. In tracing growing opposition in these chapters of Matthew, we see some of the issues facing all men—you and me as well. And we are confronted by our own necessity to choose.

ATTACK

Matthew 12

The men who seem to have spearheaded the growing opposition to Jesus were the Pharisees. Along with the Sadducees, traditionally their rivals, this band of rigid and committed men were quick to see the great gap between Israel's present life-style and Jesus' Kingdom truth.

The Pharisees. The name comes from a root meaning "separated." The movement apparently began some two centuries before Christ, and focused on resistance to Hellenization of the Jews. The Pharisees were earnestly concerned with the Law and with keeping it to the minutest detail. Strikingly, the Pharisees emphasized the "oral law" as contrasted to the "written Law" of the Torah (Pentateuch). This oral law was composed of a vast number of interpretations and explanations of the Old Testament, which over the years continued to grow and grow. Unfortunately, the oral law increasingly focused on trifling details. For instance, the command not to work on the Sabbath was expanded and illustrated with hundreds of explanations and exceptions. According to the Pharisees' oral law, a person was allowed to spit on rocky ground on the Sabbath. But he could not spit on soft or dusty earth; the spittle might move the dirt and that would constitute plowing, for it might make a furrow! Tragically, the oral law often robbed the written Law of its real message of God-like concern for other men. Jesus once rebuked the Pharisees for their practice of "giving" all of their possessions to the Temple (to be taken over after their death) and thus telling poor parents or other relatives that they owned nothing with which to help *them!* God's command to "honor your father and mother" was thus pushed aside to favor this merely human tradition.

We can see in the New Testament many evidences of the Pharisees' scrupulous concern for the minor details of legalism (Mt. 9:14; 23:16-19, 23; Lk. 11:42; Mk. 7:1-13). What we often miss is that the movement itself did have healthy roots.

The Pharisees had separated themselves from the rest of Israel because of a deep concern for righteousness. They yearned for the arrival of the Kingdom in which God and His ways would be honored in holiness. Until then, in search of personal holiness, the Pharisees joined communes of others with the same longing. Strikingly, the Pharisees were not educated or upper-class men. Instead, they were characteristically middle class and without formal education in the interpretation of the Law. In their closed communities they lived under the direction of a scribe (an expert in the Law), and there they sought to separate themselves to find righteousness through commitment to keeping the whole Law. Their commitment won them the admiration of the common people and gave this group, which in Jesus' day numbered about 6,000, great influence.

Later Paul would write something about the Jews which was characteristic of the Pharisees: "For I can testify about them that they are zealous for God, but their zeal is not based on knowledge. Since they disregarded the righteousness that comes from God and sought to establish their own, they did not submit to God's righteousness" (Rom. 10:2, 3). In their attempt to find righteousness through legalism, they missed the Old Testament's message of righteousness through faith (cf. Gen. 15:6). They became so committed to their own idea of what God's will must be that when the Son of God appeared to reveal Him, they refused to hear. For the Pharisees to respond to Jesus would have meant admitting that the principles on which they had built their lives, and which gave them their distinctive identity, had been wrong. They simply could not and would not abandon themselves, even though it was God who called.

We can sympathize with the Pharisees. Some of us, too, have had an honest concern for the things of God, but without real understanding. Jesus then confronts us and calls us to abandon all that we once held dear and true, and to rebuild our lives on

Him in ways blueprinted by the Kingdom. And we, too, hold back. Dare we surrender all we thought we had and were in order to become something new that the King commands and promises?

The Pharisees could not and would not. They insisted on holding onto their own ideas and interpretations of things rather than submitting to the King. Their rebellion not only led to their destruction, but also contributed to the suffering of the nation which they influenced.

Attack (Mt. 12:1-24). We see the Pharisee's mindset all too clearly in three incidents reported in this chapter. Walking through the grainfields, the disciples plucked and ate wheat kernels. The Pharisees shouted to Jesus, "Hey! They're breaking the Law!" They were referring to the oral law's interpretation of that act as "harvesting"—and the disciples were doing it on the Sabbath. But the Old Testament itself never interprets Sabbath Law to involve not eating.

A little later Jesus entered a synagogue of the Pharisees (12:9) where He was confronted by a man with a withered hand. This confrontation had apparently been arranged so that the Pharisees might "accuse him" (12:10). Thus they challenged Jesus: "Is it lawful to heal on the sabbath?" Jesus responded by pointing out the value of a man to God, and added, "It is lawful to do good on the Sabbath" (12:12). Jesus then healed the man—and the Pharisees went out and began to plot how to kill Jesus!

Later Jesus was seen healing, and the crowds

100

wondered aloud if He was the Messiah. Then the Pharisees, hardened in their rejection of Jesus, began their slander campaign against Him. "It is only by Beelzebul, the prince of demons, that this fellow drives out demons" (12:24).

Jesus' response (Mt. 12:25-50). Much of this chapter is devoted to Jesus' response to the attack of the Pharisees. Responding to the first attack on the disciples for plucking grain to eat as they walked, Jesus pointed out that even God's laws (to say nothing of the oral traditions!) are not meant to be rigid and unyielding rules which are exalted above human need. God is concerned with "mercy and not sacrifice." Law rightly understood is to enrich and provide a framework for love. The disciples were guiltless in this situation, and their freedom from guilt was pronounced by He who is "Lord of the Sabbath" (12:8).

The second incident also is revealing. The Pharisees were willing to use a man with a withered hand, totally unconcerned about his tragedy and his feelings, in order to try to trap Jesus! Jesus' response, affirming God's great value of the individual human being, showed up their heartlessness for what it was! No wonder they plotted to kill Him. In becoming self-righteous, the Pharisees had lost that deep concern for others which characterized God's own heart of love. Their religious zeal had, in fact, led them to become *ungodly* (un-Godlike) persons!

With their ungodliness clearly revealed in starkest contrast to the Lord's own compassion and love, the Pharisees had no choice. They had to either face their sinfulness and abandon the legalistic search for righteousness that had produced it, or strike out brutally against the one who had pierced their pretentions to reveal their lack of love. They chose to strike out.

Several important issues were raised by Jesus in the extended response that He made to the Pharisees and their followers.

The unforgivable sin. The Pharisees had rejected the evidence of Jesus' miracles and claimed that Satan's power was behind Him. This blasphemy was unique in history; never before had God's Son, standing among men as a man, by the power of God's Holy Spirit performed such obvious authenticating signs. Speaking against the source of Jesus' power was, first of all, a recognition of its supernatural origin, and second, a hardened rejection of Jesus' own explanation. Completely hardened now, this desperate attack was a demonstration of the fact that the Pharisees had made their choice. They no longer felt any hesitation at all. They were committed against the Son of God. Their choice, made in the face of all the unique evidence which Jesus Himself had presented them, was irrevocable; they had chosen to step beyond the possibility of repentance.

Idle words. Jesus spoke in 12:36 of giving account on judgment day for every "careless word" men utter. This is *not,* as some have taken it to be, a reference to chitchat in contrast to "edifying" talk about Jesus. Instead, Jesus was pointing to what is recorded in these very chapters.

The Pharisees, in reacting to the disciples' pluck-ing of the grain and in challenging Jesus concern-ing the withered hand, in the charge that He oper-ated in league with demons, had carelessly revealed their hearts! Completely unplanned by the Pharisees, what they had said expressed what was in them. No wonder verse 35 prefaces the warning about careless words with this statement: "The good man brings good things out of the good stored up in him, and the evil man brings evil things out of the evil stored up in him." What is in a man's heart will be inadvertently expressed in his words, for "out of the overflow of the heart the mouth speaks" (12:34).

We can hide our bitterness and lack of compas-sion and our hatred of others under a cloak of religiosity. We can even be rigorously "separated" from all kinds of cultural "sins." But when our reac-tions and our words reveal a Pharisee-like con-tempt for men and women whom God loves, our ungodliness is revealed.

The section of dialogue closes with Jesus' refusal to give Israel any more miraculous signs as proof of His identity, and with a renewed warning that judgment must surely come. Nineveh, a pagan land, responded to Jonah's preaching. The pagan Queen of Sheba responded to Solomon's instruc-tion. But Israel had refused to respond to Jesus, though He is greater by far than either Jonah or Solomon.

By turning away the King, Israel opened them-selves up to utter emptiness and a terrifying fate.

103

No longer could physical descent from Abraham be considered a mark of standing with God. Each individual had to see that his relationship was personal, and would hinge on doing the will of the Father in Heaven (12:46-50).

THE PARABLES

Matthew 13

The same day that Jesus spoke out warning His hearers of the tragedy which rejection of the King and Kingdom was to bring upon them, He sat in a boat to teach the gathering crowds. The Bible says He "told them many things in parables" (13:3).

There is a multitude of parables in the Bible. The word itself means to "set alongside," and it is a normal pattern of Scripture to illustrate by setting concrete and familiar illustrations alongside abstract concepts (cf. II Sam. 12:1-7; Jdg. 9:8-15; and Isa. 5:1-7 for Old Testament examples). Sometimes parables are allegories, such as the story of the good Samaritan through which Jesus answered the man who wondered aloud, "Who is my neighbor?"

But there is something very different about the parables recorded in Matthew 13. Rather than illuminating what Jesus said, they almost seem to obscure it!

Why then did Jesus speak in parables? There are several hints in the text. Asked this question by the disciples, Jesus said, "Though seeing, they do not

FIGURE V

PARABLES OF THE KINGDOM

THE PARABLE	EXPECTED FORM	UNEXPECTED CHARACTERISTIC
1. *sower* 13:3-9, 18-23	Messiah turns *Israel* and all *nations* to Himself.	*Individuals* respond differently to the Word's invitation.
2. *wheat/tares* 13:24-30, 37-43	The Kingdom's righteous citizens *rule* over the world with the King.	The Kingdom's citizens are *among* the men of the world, growing together till God's harvesttime.
3. *mustard seed* 13:31-32	Kingdom *begins* in *majestic glory.*	Kingdom *begins in insignificance;* its greatness comes as a surprise.
4. *leaven* 13:33	Only righteousness enters the Kingdom; other "raw material" is excluded.	The Kingdom is implanted in a different "raw material" and grows to fill the whole personality with righteousness.
5. *hidden treasure* 13:44	Kingdom is *public* and for all.	Kingdom is *hidden* and for individual "purchase."
6. *priceless pearl* 13:45, 46	Kingdom *brings all valued things* to men.	Kingdom demands *abandonment* of all other values (cf. Mt. 6:33).
7. *dragnet* 13:47-50	Kingdom begins with initial separation of righteous and unrighteous.	Kingdom ends with final separation of the unrighteous from the righteous.

105

see; though hearing they do not hear, or understand" (13:13). The crowds, in rejecting Jesus' clear teaching about the Kingdom and His presentation of Himself as King, had closed their eyes to truth. Now Jesus would speak less clear words to them, lest they be even more responsible!

It is also possible that Jesus adapted parables here to keep the listeners concentrating on the choice they had to make for or against Him. We need to remember that the Israelites had a clear notion of what the Kingdom would be like. They would not be shaken from this single conception to accept additional truth which modified their expectations. Jesus later explained to His disciples that the parables were spoken for *them* (13:16), and that they dealt with a dimension of the Kingdom which was not the subject of earlier Old Testament revelation. The parables, Jesus explained, fulfilled this prophecy:

I will open my mouth in parables;
I will utter things hidden since the
    creation of the world.

Matthew 13:35

These parables deal with dimensions of the Kingdom which Israel did not suspect existed. They deal, in fact, with those dimensions of the Kingdom which you and I experience today and will experience until, at the return of Christ, the Old Testament's prophesied Kingdom rule *is* established forever.

No wonder the disciples, themselves steeped in the Old Testament's lore, were also puzzled and had to ask Jesus, "Explain to us the parable of the weeds in the field" (13:36). Only later could they look back and see in Jesus' words the portrait of a time between the Lord's Resurrection and the establishment of the earthly Kingdom in its expected form. These, then, are parables of contrast. By contrast they illuminate key differences between the prophesied Kingdom reign and the present servant form of the Kingdom over which Jesus now rules.

Jesus concluded His seven parables with a question: "Have you understood all these things?" (13:51). Afraid to say no, the twelve nodded "Yes." Both the old and the new are elements in the Kingdom which Christ came to bring. Only later would they begin to understand the deep implications for the Church of the unexpected form of Kingdom about which Jesus spoke.

RESISTANCE

Matthew 13:53–15:20

The failure to respond to Jesus was becoming open resistance to Him and His teachings. When Jesus returned to His hometown, He was resented rather than honored (13:57).

John's death at the hands of Herod (14:1-12) added its dampening effect. The early mood of expectancy with which Jesus' ministry had been met was evaporating. The Pharisees had taken sides against Him. He had not acted like the expected King. The hated Herod had even executed His cousin John—and Jesus had done nothing. Instead of mounting a vengeful attack on Herod and Rome, Jesus "withdrew . . . to a solitary place" (14:13).

The crowds followed Him. Waiting. Although Jesus would no longer perform miracles as authenticating signs to demonstrate the validity of His claim, He still was moved by compassion for human need. Jesus continued to heal because He cared. Then, with the crowds hungry and no source of food nearby, Jesus distributed a multiplied five loaves and two fish to the thousands who had come.

Late that night He met His disciples on the sea (14:22-32). They'd taken a boat; He walked across the waters to them. The rejecting Pharisees and doubting crowd would receive no more proof of His authority. But the believing disciples would continue to receive miraculous reassurance. So it is even today. The evidence men seek—and then reject when given—is withheld. But the believer who walks with Jesus sees constant evidence that God is ever near.

This section of the story of Jesus closes with the Pharisees returning to Jesus once again. Hating Him as they did, they still seemed driven to come and, through confrontation, to find some justification for their stand.

Again the Pharisees attacked at a point developed in the oral law. "Why do your disciples break the tradition of the elders? They don't wash their hands [ceremonially] before they eat!" (15:2).

Again Jesus bluntly confronted them, seeking to reveal the emptiness and hypocrisy they had substituted for the heart of God's revealed Law.

"Why do you break the command of God for the sake of your tradition?" (vs. 3), He asked. Their whole approach to life "invalidated the word of God" (vs. 6, NASB) for the sake of their tradition; they were setting aside the intention of God for the sake of a legalistic self-righteousness! Lashing out at these religious men, Jesus cried, "You hypocrites! Isaiah was right when he prophesied about you:"

> These people honor me with their lips,
>   but their hearts are far from me.
> They worship me in vain;
>   their teachings are but rules made by man.
> *Matthew 15:7-9*

And again Jesus focused attention on the heart (15:10-20). It is not what a man eats or how he washes that defiles. It is the heart of man that defiles and it is this with which the King and Kingdom deal. Only Jesus can heal the diseased heart, and His work is done within.

Coming to the Kingdom, we must abandon all that we have relied on to perfect ourselves. We must abandon all we are into the hands of the King. We may, like Israel, long for the outward pomp and glory of God's future power. Yet, we must surrender all this for now. If we recognize Jesus as our

King, He must be given our individual personality over which to reign.

GOING DEEPER

to personalize

1. From Matthew 12 and information in the text, in what ways might a tendency to Pharisaism show in believers today?

2. Examine Matthew 23. From Matthew 12 and 23 and 15:1-9, what do you see as the basic fault of Pharisaism? What is its corrective?

3. Look at the parables (Mt. 13) and the parables chart on page 105. Select *one* of the longer parables and, following the interpretation approach suggested in the text, write a two-page paper on "the meaning of this parable for me today."

4. In two extended segments, Matthew 13:33-37 and 15:10-20, Jesus discussed the heart. Look at them carefully, and in one *sentence* summarize the point Jesus was making.

to probe

1. Research the Pharisees, their origins, teachings, life-style, influence in Israel, etc.

2. Research the parables. What are parables? How are they used in Scripture? What kinds of subjects do they cover? How do various commentators interpret these unusual parables contained in Matthew 13?

BY FAITH:
THE TURNING POINT

THIS AFTERNOON on a flight to Denver I sat next
to a rabinnical student from Orthodox Judaism. As
we talked it became clear that I was seated beside a
worthy successor of the Pharisees. Like them, he
believed that the oral law was given at Sinai, that
the complete Jewish faith and life-style were communicated then and never have been modified
since. He challenged me about the very incident
which we looked at in chapter 7: the time when the
disciples plucked wheat and ate on the Sabbath. I
explained Jesus' response: that the oral law is
human tradition. As Lord of the Sabbath, Jesus rejected these incorporations which actually robbed
the Law of its meaning and intent.

He smiled. Clearly his confidence that he had the
entire truth was as unshaken as had been the assur-

ance of the Pharisees of Jesus' day. The way of the Law was the way of life.

Assurance that one knows the whole truth about God's plans and intentions, and that there can be no possible variations which we have not understood, is always a dangerous thing. If you and I adopt this attitude, we shut ourselves off from new insights from the Word of God and are in danger of shutting out God's Spirit as He seeks to teach us. When we close our minds and hearts and insist that we have all truth, any suggestion of new truth frightens and shakes us.

We can understand, then, that what we are about to see in Matthew 15—17 had great potential to disturb both Jesus' countrymen and His disciples. Jesus went on to further explain the unexpected form of the Kingdom which His death and Resurrection would install and which He had already introduced (in Mt. 13).

Let's trace through what we've seen in Matthew to date, and note how a definite shift in Jesus' Kingdom teaching was taking place. Note the key points on Figure III, p. 33.

As opposition grew, that particular expression of the Kingdom for which the Jews looked receded. Increasingly Jesus began to speak about an expression of God's Kingdom on earth which was unexpected: that which had been "hidden since the creation of the world" (Mt. 13:35).

The point of national decision seems to have been reached with an event recorded in Matthew 16:13-21. Great crowds had continued to come to hear Jesus and to rejoice in His healings (15:31). In Caesarea Philippi, Jesus asked His disciples, "Who do people say the Son of Man is?" (16:13). The disciples reported a variety of reactions. Some thought Jesus was John the Baptist come back; others suggested Elijah or Jeremiah or another of the ancient prophets. This was high praise! Clearly Jesus was regarded as one who was under the blessing and authority of God. But still Israel did not recognize Jesus as the promised Messiah and Son of God. They would not bow down to their King!

Jesus then turned to His disciples and asked, "Who do you say I am?" (16:15). Peter answered for the twelve: "You are the Christ [Messiah], the Son of the living God" (16:16). It is upon this foundation—recognition of Jesus Christ as both Messiah and Son of the living God—that any expression of the Kingdom must be based. On this foundation, Jesus said, "I will build my church" (16:18). Then Jesus charged the disciples to tell no one that He was the Christ and, the Bible says, "From that time on Jesus began to explain to his disciples that he must go to Jerusalem and suffer many things . . . and . . . be killed, and on the third day be raised" (16:21).

From that time the message of the "Kingdom at Hand" was subordinated to the message of the Cross. From this point also the Book of Matthew shows a definite shift in emphasis. Jesus increasingly stressed principles on which the present (between Resurrection and return) form of the Kingdom would operate.

FOCUS ON FAITH
Matthew 15:21–16:12

The section begins with a significant incident. Jesus was confronted by a Canaanite woman who pleaded with Him to heal her daughter. Jesus refused, saying, "I was sent only to the lost sheep of Israel" (15:24). This is a tremendously significant saying. What's more, it is not an isolated statement! When Jesus gave authority to the twelve to preach and heal, He told them, "Do not go among the Gentiles or enter any town of the Samaritans. Go rather to the lost sheep of Israel" (10:5, 6).

This, of course, fit the expectations of the Jews. They knew that they were God's chosen people. As the seed of Abraham, they were possessors of God's Covenant promises. When the Messiah came, He would reestablish the Davidic kingdom and rule from Jerusalem, regathering all Israel to share His glory with them. Of course, with the kingdom established, the knowledge of God would fill the earth. Then even the Gentile nations would look to the Messiah (see Isa. 11). But the Messiah was *Israel's* King. Just as Israel belongs to God in a special way (Hos. 11:1-5; Mic. 6:3-5), so the Messiah belongs to Israel (Mic. 4:1-5; Jer. 31). Until rejected by the people of Israel, Jesus conscientiously made Himself available to them. John puts it this way: "He came to that which was his own, but his own did not receive him" (Jn. 1:11).

Strikingly, the Canaanite woman recognized Jesus for who He was. She addressed Him, "Lord,

114

Son of David," giving Him His Messianic title. Rebuked by Jesus, she asked for the crumbs which, overflowing from Israel's future table, would bless the world. Jesus answered, "Woman, you have great faith! Your request is granted" (Mt. 15:28).

The Kingdom benefits which Israel as a nation rejected when she refused to recognize her King would now be made available to all men—on the basis of faith.

Matthew 15:29—16:12 continues to portray Jesus as offering Himself to Israel. He healed, He fed the crowds, He continued to warn against the Pharisees who had been unable to interpret the many signs proving the King's presence.

And then Jesus asked the fateful question: "Who do men say that the Son of man is?" And the disciples' report confirmed what had already been made clear. The nation had rejected Jesus. Peter's confession of faith, "You are the Christ, the Son of the living God" (16:16), was a confession which Israel could not and would not make.

REFOCUSED

Matthew 16:13-28

These few verses, coming as they do at the turning point in Matthew's portrait of the life of Christ, have been an object of controversy through much of Church history. What is the foundation on which the Church will be built? What are the "keys of the kingdom" (16:19) that Jesus gave Peter? What are the denial of self and the taking up of one's cross which Jesus said enable a person to find himself?

The foundation (Mt. 16:17, 18). After Peter's affirmation, Jesus called Peter blessed. God had revealed Christ's identity to him. And Jesus went on to say, "On this rock I will build my church" (16:18).

The ancient Church fathers gave various interpretations of this statement. Some said that the rock on which the Church was founded was Peter. Others insisted that the name Peter (which means "little stone") hardly could be identified as a foundation rock. Other fathers have argued that the Church is founded on Peter's *confession:* it is the faith in Christ that Peter professed which is the Church's foundation. Still others have seen this as a reference to Christ Himself: Jesus the Christ, the Son of God, is the foundation.

The Epistles seem to support this third conclusion. "No one can lay any foundation other than the one already laid," says I Corinthians 3:11, "which is Jesus Christ." Christ Himself, the Messiah and Son of God, is the foundation of the Church and Kingdom.

The keys (Mt. 16:19). What then about the gift of the "keys of the kingdom" and the promise that "whatever you bind on earth will be bound in heaven, and whatever you loose on earth will be loosed in heaven"? What are the keys, and what are loosing and binding?

Here again there have been disagreements. To some these verses are clear evidence that the

Church, as made visible in the Roman pontiff, is the "Vicar of Christ on earth." It is believed that the power of making binding decisions has been dele-- gated to Peter and his successors. But this notion came late in Church history, after the bishop of Rome gained dominance over the other bishoprics.

Other scholars have noted that Peter was chosen by God to open the door of the Gospel to each of the two major groups of mankind recognized in his day. At Pentecost, Peter preached the first Gospel sermon to the Jews. Later still, God chose him to speak to Cornelius, the first Gentile to become a part of the Body of Christ (Acts 10, 11). Yet, this does not explain binding and loosing.

One thing is clear in the New Testament: Jesus is Head over all things for the Church which is His Body (Eph. 2:22). Jesus was not surrendering His position to any individual or group of men. If we realize our direct involvement with Jesus as our Head, this will suggest the best solution to the puzzle. How do we on earth speak with such authority? Only because we on earth are, through Jesus' presence within us, an extension of Christ Himself. Our Head, who directs us, acts through His Body on earth to loose and bind authoritatively. How fully, then, you and I need to be committed to Christ's lordship, and how fully we need to obey him! As believers respond to Jesus' direction, the Kingdom continues to express its presence on earth.

Jesus' response to the disciples' confession was pointed and striking. He confirmed their awareness that He is the Messiah and Son of God, and

117

announced His intention of building on this reality a "Church," literally a "called-out assembly." Moreover, this Church is to be the lived-out expression of Heaven on earth. In our relationship with Jesus we are to express the Kingdom in our generation's "here and now." The destiny of the believer goes beyond Israel's dream of being citizens of the Kingdom. The destiny of the believer is to *express* the Kingdom. We bind and loose; we affirm forgiveness of sin and its retention. We speak God's Word, not on our authority, but on the authority Christ shares with us as He shared it with those disciples He once sent out two by two (Mt. 10).

The portrait given here is an overwhelming one. To *be* the Kingdom! To reflect Jesus in our world! To express Him, His grace and judgments! This is who we are called to be—and become.

This is who we are.

To become (Mt. 16:24-28). Realizing that as Kingdom citizens we are to reflect the King may make us feel guilty or unworthy. It is not meant to. Instead, it is meant to help us sense our calling and to respond joyfully to follow our Lord. There *is* a gap between our present experience and our calling. Recognizing the gap, Jesus told His disciples, "If anyone would come after me . . ." (16:24). If we want to follow Jesus, we are invited to, and are shown the results!

The results? "Whoever loses his life for me will find it" (16:25). This puzzling statement is made more clear when we realize that the word translated "life" here, and "soul" in some translations, reflects a common Hebrew and Greek usage. The words *nephesh* (Hebrew) and *psuche* (Greek) can mean "soul" or "life." But they are often used as a reflexive pronoun. Thus, Jesus warned not of losing one's life, but of losing *oneself*. "Whoever loses himself for me," Jesus was saying, "will find himself." And "what good will it be for a man if he gains the whole world yet forfeits his . . . [self]?" (16:26). What self was Jesus speaking of here? Jesus was speaking of the persons you and I can become as disciples who choose to follow Him.

You and I *can* choose to turn away from all that the Kingdom citizenship offers. If we do, we will never become the persons that Jesus yearns to make us. Or we can follow Jesus and lose the self we are—that self that feels guilt and shame for all failures. In following Jesus you can become the person you yearn to be.

What does it take? How do we follow Jesus? "He must deny himself and take up his cross and follow me" (16:24). Each of these three is significant:

Self-denial. It would be a mistake to see self-denial as denying oneself pleasures or joys. The Bible says that God "giveth us richly all things to enjoy" (I Tim. 6:17, KJV). And one of the Pharisees' criticisms of Jesus was that He went to parties! No, self-denial is far more significant than this. It involves a denial of the values, the attitudes, and the emotions of which Jesus spoke in the Beatitudes. For example, bitterness is rooted in the old self and is to be denied. When Christ speaks to us when we are bitter, insisting that we let forgiveness wash

119

away the bitterness, all that's old in us fights against that action. Pride, competitiveness, and self-pity all struggle within to direct our reaction. To deny these natural pressures within ourselves involves denying the self that we are in order to follow Jesus and choose the self He alone can help us become.

Daily cross. It is significant that Jesus did not ask us to take up *His* Cross. Instead, He teaches us to be willing to take up *our* cross daily. Why a cross? Not because of suffering, but because the Cross speaks of Jesus' willing choice of that which was God's will for Him. It is the daily choice of God's will for us—whatever His will may prove to be—to which Jesus calls us as His disciples.

Follow Me. This is the heart of Jesus' invitation to us. Follow. But not at a distance. Not as someone searching for tracks to trace a figure long disappeared over the horizon. No, Jesus' "Follow Me" means *"Keep close* to Me." Only when we are close to Jesus can we find the strength for self-denial, and only when we are close to Jesus can we sense His daily guidance of our life.

Denying the old self, choosing daily the Father's will, and keeping close to Jesus, we will—as the first disciples did—find our true selves.

COMING GLORY

Matthew 17

Jesus' talk of His coming death was deeply disturbing to the disciples (16:22, 23). Disturbing, too, was the choice Jesus then set before them: "If any-one would come after me . . ." (16:24). There was no overpowering coming here, sweeping all Israel into a promised glory. Instead, each individual had to face his own private choice: "Shall I follow the King?" The pathway on which the King walked, a way of self-denial and a daily cross, was tremendously less appealing than the expected Old Testament Kingdom!

Yet, Matthew 16 closes with Jesus making another puzzling statement: "Some who are standing here will not taste death before they see the Son of Man coming in his kingdom" (vs. 28). The next verse says, "After six days Jesus took with him Peter, James, and John . . . and led them up a high mountain by themselves" (17:1). Some of the disciples, but not all, were about to see the glory they will share when Jesus comes into His promised Kingdom.

There on the mountain Jesus was "transfigured before them. His face shone like the sun, and his clothes became as white as the light" (17:2). There, too, appeared Moses (who had died) and Elijah (who had been taken up into Heaven without passing through death) to talk with Him. The present pathway for Jesus led to the Cross, *but the Cross was the doorway to glory.*

On the way down the mountain, Jesus warned the three disciples not to share this experience with anyone until He had been raised from the dead. Impressed by the vision and eager for that time of glory to arrive, they seemed disturbed by the fact

121

that Elijah, the forerunner, hadn't accompanied them. They asked, "Why then do the teachers of the law say that [before the Messianic Kingdom is established] Elijah must come first?" (17:10). Jesus answered that Elijah will come first (vs. 11), and that if Israel had responded to Jesus, John the Baptist's ministry would have been considered the fulfillment to the Elijah prophecy.

As they were coming down from the mountain, a crowd led by a man with an epileptic son met Jesus and the three disciples (17:14-20). The other disciples had tried to cure the son but had failed. Now the father appealed to Jesus. And Jesus responded. The faithless and perverse generation rejected Jesus as King—and yet constantly sought His help.

Later the disciples asked Jesus why they had been powerless to help. Jesus answered, "Because you have so little faith" (17:20). The people of Israel, because of faithlessness, were unable to enter the Kingdom. And the disciples, who had entered the Kingdom through recognition of the King, were unable to experience Kingdom power for the same fault: lack of faith.

To enter the Kingdom and to live victoriously in it, faith is required.

The last incident (17:24-27) sums up in a unique way the message Jesus had begun to communicate to His unresponsive people. The Old Testament established a half-shekel tax to be paid to the Temple by each adult male. Confronted by the tax collectors, Peter was asked if Jesus paid the tax. He blurted out, "Yes."

At home, Jesus asked Peter, "From whom do the kings of the earth collect duty and taxes—from their own sons or from others?" (17:25). Peter gave the obvious answer: "From others." "Then," said Jesus, "the sons are exempt."

What was Jesus' point? The Jews had assumed that because they were the physical descendants of Abraham, they had a special relationship with God and claim on Him. But the very fact that God taxed the Jews for Temple maintenance demonstrated clearly that they were *not* sons! The physical basis on which the Israelites thought they could claim relationship with God was inadequate, and it had always been so. The men who so proudly claimed Abraham as their father (Jn. 8:33-41) had failed to realize that Abraham's relationship with God had been rooted in faith, not in the Law. They rejected that very quality of the man, whose descendants they claimed to be, which made him God's man.

Without faith, that generation lost for Israel and mankind the very Kingdom whose living expression you and I are today called to be.

By faith.

GOING DEEPER

to personalize

1. There are several difficult sayings of Jesus here which must be understood in the context of the passage. Look at them and jot down your explanation.

123

(a) "It is not right to take the children's bread and toss it to their dogs" (15:26).

(b) Out of my sight, Satan! You are a stumbling block to me; you do not have in mind the things of God, but the things of men" (16:23).

(c) "O unbelieving and perverse generation, how long shall I stay with you? How long shall I put up with you?" (17:17).

2. How was Jesus' anger at the Pharisees' seeking of a sign (miracle) related to the emphasis of these chapters (see 16:1-4)? How does it relate to us today?

3. How is your daily cross the "doorway to glory" for you (see p. 120)?

4. Select any paragraph from this section of Scripture and write briefly on its meaning for the people of Jesus' day, and then on its meaning for us today.

5. Master the chart on page 196, which will help you think through Matthew without using any other aids.

to probe

1. Check commentaries for several various interpretations of the "keys of the kingdom" and the "loose and bind" sayings of Jesus (Mt. 16:19).

2. Check to see which of the early church fathers argued for each of the three different viewpoints sketched in the text (p. 116).

3. In chapter 7 we noted how the parables of Matthew 13 show a shift from the Old Testament

picture of the expected Kingdom to an unexpected form. Make a chart to show additional contrasts which seem to you to be emphasized in Matthew 15—17.

TOWARD GREATNESS

SOMETIMES WE APOLOGIZE for dreaming great dreams. As a young Christian, I had dreams of becoming another apostle Paul, fully dedicated to Christ and the Gospel. My dreams were foolish. But I'm sure they were not wrong.

Neither were the disciples wrong when they came to Jesus to ask about greatness. "Who is the greatest in the kingdom of heaven?" (18:1) they inquired. Their simple question launched a series of teachings and events which show us in a unique way just how different spiritual greatness is from all that we expect.

It's all right for you and me to want to be great. But we must first grasp what greatness *is*. The vision we often have, looking up to the famous preacher holding crowds spellbound, or the sensitive counselor whom all respect, or the brilliant teacher everyone flocks to hear, can actually blind us. Actually a journey toward greatness is a journey down.

FIRST STEPS

Matthew 18

The disciples' request to know who is greatest in the Kingdom stimulated a totally unexpected reply. "He called a little child and had him stand among them. And he said: 'I tell you the truth, unless you change and become like little children, you will never enter the kingdom of heaven' " (18:2, 3).

Faith (Mt. 18:1-6). The child is the living embodiment of several truths which His disciples had missed. The first truth involves faith, a theme developed in chapters 15—17. Seeking greatness, the disciples were to humble themselves as one of the little ones "who believe in me."

The people of Israel did not respond when Jesus called them to Him. They stood off at a distance, reserving judgment. When Jesus called the child to Him, the child responded immediately. Without pride, humble and trusting, the child accepted Jesus' invitation at once.

Greatness comes only when we humble ourselves to trustingly respond to our King's every call.

Concern for "little ones" (Mt. 18:6-35). Jesus then lashed out at those who cause these little ones to sin (18:6-9). This world is the kind of place in which temptations to sin are bound to come, but little ones are to be protected and received. So Jesus warned, "See that you do not look down on one of these little ones" (18:10).

These three following illustrations show how to care for Christ's little ones:

Matthew 18:10-14. Like sheep, little ones who go astray are to be searched for and restored to the fold. The Palestinian shepherd gave each sheep in his flock a name, and knew each individually. Rather than driving his flock, the shepherd led. The sheep, knowing his voice, followed him (cf. Jn. 10:3). When a young lamb wandered away, the shepherd left the flock in the sheepfold and braved any weather to find the lost one. Climbing over rocks, searching each crevasse, the shepherd gave himself freely to find the lost one. Finding it, the shepherd had no thought of punishment, but only joy that the lost one was restored.

Faith does not make you or me great. It makes us one of God's little ones, sheep who need a shepherd's care.

Matthew 18:15-22. Here Jesus changed the simile. Little ones are sheep—but little ones are also brothers.

"If your brother sins against you, go and show him his fault" (18:15), Jesus began. Temptations to sin must surely come, as Jesus had already pointed out (18:7). Even with men of faith, sin will intrude, with all its hurts and pain, to break the fellowship of the family. Such failings are not to break the family unity. A brotherly desire for reconciliation can keep God's little ones from turning away from Him.

This troubled Peter, who asked, "How many times shall I forgive my brother when he sins against me? Up to seven times?" (18:21). Christ's answer: "Seventy times seven" (i.e., "always")!

Faith does not lift us above the possibility of sin. But forgiveness can cancel sin's impact on family relationships.

Matthew 18:23-35. Once again the simile shifted. Here, we the little ones are seen as servants. Christ, our King, has forgiven us a great debt. In His patience and love, He treats us gently and lovingly. As servants of such a King, we are now called on to have patience with our fellow believers (18:29). Failure to have such patience and to extend forgiveness will cut us off from the experience of God's own forgiveness.

Faith does not elevate our status; we become servants! And we are to treat our fellow servants as God treats us.

Greatness? The disciples must have been stunned by this discourse. They had asked about greatness, but Jesus had spoken only about God's little ones! They had been thinking of great deeds and high thrones, but Jesus had spoken of sheep and brothers and servants. What did all this have to do with greatness?

Much, for them and for us. To be great in Christ's present Kingdom, you and I must first of all take our place as God's little ones—and learn to see our fellow believers in the same way. In our desire to excel, we must never forget that we are sheep, prone to go astray, always in need of our Shepherd's tender care. We must never forget that all other Christians are brothers, and seek to live in fullest harmony with them. We must never forget that we are simply servants living with (not over) fellow servants. And we must treat all others with that same patience and forgiveness which Jesus shows us.

One of the most poignant passages in Scripture pictures the apostle Paul ministering to God's little ones. Paul reminds the Thessalonians:

> We were gentle among you, like a mother caring for her little children. We loved you so much that we were delighted to share with you not only the gospel of God but our lives as well, because you had become so dear to us . . . you know that we dealt with each of you as a father deals with his own children, encouraging, comforting and urging you to live lives worthy of God, who calls you into his kingdom and glory.
>
> *I Thessalonians 2:7-12*

Do you want to be great? Then take your place among God's little ones, and love them into Christ's Kingdom.

ANOTHER WAY?

Matthew 19:1–20:16

Jesus' ideas about greatness are revolutionary. Soon they were contrasted against the ideas of the religious men of His day, ideas still popular today. And still wrong.

The way of the Law (Mt. 19:3-5). The Pharisees are still the classic example of persons zealous for God

131

who seek to find spiritual greatness by rigid adherence to both Biblical and human standards of righteousness. These proponents of strict legalism appeared to test Jesus, apparently bringing up a subject which Jesus has spoken on before. "Is it lawful for a man to divorce his wife for any and every reason?" (19:3). Jesus' answer goes back to the Creation account. He pointed out that God intended marriage to unite two persons as one; thus divorce is not His intention.

Immediately the Pharisees struck back. "Why then did Moses command that a man give his wife a certificate of divorce" (19:7)? The Law permitted divorce. Jesus' answer had to be wrong.

Christ's response reveals the root of legalism's error: "Moses permitted you to divorce your wives because your hearts were hard" (19:8). Rather than being a way to a superior righteousness, the Law involves an accommodation to weakness and sin! The Pharisees' legalism even led them to ask the wrong question. They did not ask, "How can we restore the broken relationships which bring agony into marriage?" No, they asked instead, "Is it all right to deepen the hurt by making the alienation permanent!" They did not care about broken hearts crushed by rejection. They took refuge instead in an exception, permitted by the Law because they were too hardhearted to care!

The disciples themselves missed the point. Jesus had just taught them about greatness, and shown that true greatness is to restore the straying lamb, to exercise constant patience, and to continue to be

132

ready to forgive. Others, too, are God's little ones, and may need years of tender love to help them grow. Failing to relate Christ's teaching on greatness to this legal issue, the disciples blurted out instead, "In that case, it's better not to marry!" Even they were unwilling to totally commit themselves to another person without reserve.

Jesus' answer to the disciples was that not to marry was, indeed, God's will for some but for "only those to whom it has been given" (19:11). But He added, "The one who can accept this should accept it" (19:12).

Again Jesus drew children around Him. "Let the little children come to me, and do not hinder them," He said to His disciples (19:14). Let's take our place as children gladly, realizing that Jesus welcomes us—and commands us not to hinder others' freedom to come.

The way of "goodness" (Mt. 19:16–20:16). Immediately after this a young man came up to Jesus and asked, "What good thing must I do to get eternal life?" (19:16). This young man was a good person, one whose goodness was expressed in his honest observation of the Law. But Jesus challenged him on one point. "Sell your possessions and give to the poor, and . . . come, follow me" (19:21).

The young man turned away.

No. This was not a universal command to all the rich. Instead, it was a challenge to this individual who measured his goodness by his dealings with other men. Yet, this humanistic benevolence avoids the first commandment: "You shall have no other

133

gods before Me" (Ex. 20:3, NASB). Jesus' words
were a command from His God. Hearing them, the
young man rebelled in order to choose his wealth.
All human goodness fails at this same point. It is
good to do good to others, but it is not enough. God
must be the focus of our lives.

As the young man walked sadly away, Jesus remarked that wealth makes it difficult to enter the
Kingdom. The disciples, who, like others in their
culture, viewed wealth as evidence of God's favor,
asked in astonishment, "Who then can be saved?"
The answer? "With man this is impossible, but with
God all things are possible" (Mt. 19:25, 26).

At this point, Peter blurted out yet another foolish question. The disciples had left all to follow
Jesus. What would they gain? Jesus accommodated
His answer to their need. They were still concerned
about the kind of greatness that involves status and
power. Jesus reassured them: "At the renewal of all
things, when the Son of Man sits on his throne in
heavenly glory, you who have followed me will also
sit on twelve thrones, judging the twelve tribes of
Israel" (19:28). But, Jesus added, *This is not for now!*
For now "many who are first will be last, and many
who are last will be first" (19:30).

The way of hard work (Mt. 20:1-16). A final parable
was added to explain the "last first" comment. Jesus
pictured a landowner who went out early in the
morning and hired men to work in his harvest.
Later he went out and found more standing idle.
He sent them into his fields as well. Several times
during the day this pattern was repeated.

At evening, those who had worked the full day were dismayed to find that those who had worked only two hours received as much pay as they! When they complained, the landowner explained that they were paid what they had agreed on that morning. As for the rest, their reward was a matter not of what had been earned, but what was given by the owner out of generosity. The last had been first.

Like each of the workers in Jesus' parable, we have been invited to serve in His Kingdom. What is important is our response to the King when He calls us to our individual task. Greatness is not measured by how long or hard we may try to work to gain reward.

Greg found this out at a Faith/at/Work retreat. For eight years he directed an evangelistic mission which flooded 70 countries with college students. He labored 16 and 18 hours a day, and his feeling of worth and value was directly tied to the length of his day. At the retreat, Greg was confronted by a small group who revealed that they saw him as a man with a "Messiah complex," someone who thought he was called to save the world all by himself. Greg broke into tears. For the first time he realized that all his Christian life he had been trying to earn God's favor, caught up in an endless struggle for acceptance. During that week, Greg discovered that he *is* one of God's little ones.

Currently a pastor in Colorado, Greg is now free to respond when God calls, and is finding a rich reward in the conversion and growth of many whom the Lord touches through him.

In the Kingdom of Christ's present reign we *are* called to greatness. But we will not find it on some of those roads the religious of the ages have traveled. Christ has another way, marked out for all of us who humbly accept our place as His trusting little ones.

THE SERVANT LEADER

Matthew 20:17-28

Again Jesus took the twelve aside and spoke to them of His death. "We are going up to Jerusalem, and the Son of Man will be betrayed to the chief priests and the teachers of the law. They will condemn him to death and will turn him over to the Gentiles to be mocked and flogged and crucified. On the third day be will be raised to life!" (20:17-19). In the context of teaching on greatness, Jesus focused the attention of His disciples on His own choice to give His life.

We see why. Immediately afterward, the mother of James and John, two of the twelve, came to Jesus to ask for the right- and left-hand seats in the coming Kingdom for her sons. These two seats represent power and honor. Momma was politicking for her boys.

It's clear from the context that James and John had asked her to intercede, and were standing close by to hear the Lord's answer. "You don't know what you are asking," was Jesus' weary reply. "Can you," He said, turning to the two listening disciples, "drink the cup I am going to drink?" (20:22). Authority and power in the Kingdom are not what the disciples imagined. The leader will influence others, but he will perform his ministry in the same way that Jesus chose to perform His. Still not understanding, James and John eagerly insisted that they were able to drink Jesus' cup. "You will do that," Jesus replied. But the power and position they yearned for was something Jesus would not promise.

When the other ten disciples heard, they were indignant at James and John. So Jesus called all twelve around Him, and gave them what is probably the most significant instruction recorded in the New Testament about spiritual leadership:

> You know that the rulers of the Gentiles lord it over them, and their high officials exercise authority over them. Not so with you. Instead, whoever wants to become great among you must be your servant, and whoever wants to be first must be your slave—just as the Son of Man did not come to be served, but to serve, and to give his life a ransom for many.
> *Matthew 20:25-28*

In this short passage, Jesus once and for all put to rest the pretensions of the spiritual leaders of every age to that kind of "power" that demands the right to command.

The secular ruler. Jesus set up two models or examples of leaders. The one model is provided by

137

the secular ruler of Jesus' day, the emperor or king or governor who "exercises authority over" others. There are many characteristics of this style of leadership, some made explicit in the text and some implicit in the example chosen.

For instance, there is a distinctive relationship between the leader and the led; the secular leader "exercises authority *over*." When I was in the Navy, my commanding officer, Lieutenant Kahle, was about five feet two inches tall, a full foot shorter than I. It was the most peculiar sensation, standing in front of Lieutenant Kahle and still feeling that I was looking up! There is a relational distance between the leader and the led in the secular world.

Another significant characteristic is implied in both the phrases "lord it over them" and "exercise authority." The secular ruler has the ability to enforce his will. He has sanctions to make sure that his orders are obeyed. This was certainly true in my Navy days. If I had not responded, my liberty (time off) could have been canceled. I could have been taken to captain's mast (informal court). I could have been court-martialed. Punishments ranging from restriction to the base, to the forfeiture of my pay, to imprisonment assured my conformity. Secular leaders have this kind of power.

A third significant characteristic implicit in both the above has to do with *how* leadership is exercised. From his position above, using his power to enforce, the secular ruler *leads by command*. He simply tells others what to do, and they do it.

The servant leader. Jesus chose a servant as the

countermodel for His followers. Nothing could be farther from our idea of greatness or leadership. We tend to see as did the disciples, the pomp of power. The TV cameras focus in on the great seal of the United States, a hushed quiet falls, the band in the background plays "Hail to the Chief," and the announcer's voice is heard: "Ladies and gentlemen: The President of the United States." We feel that is greatness. That is what being a leader is all about.

And then Jesus directs our attention to a quiet man standing off camera, a man in overalls with the working tools of his trade. And Jesus says that is greatness! That is what being a leader is all about.

This graphic contrast must have jolted the disciples just as it jolts us. Yet Jesus clearly wants us to see each of these persons as leaders. Each of them is to be seen as having authority and the power to move other men. What, then, are the significant contrasts between the two?

While the secular ruler is above those he leads, Jesus said, "Not so with you" (20:26). Instead of relational distance, there is relational closeness. The Christian leader must seek to be one with the people he is called to serve.

Instead of "exercising authority" as a ruler who demands and enforces conformity, the Christian leader is to be cut off from coercion. Jesus said firmly and plainly: *"Not so with you."* Force, manipulation, demand—all are ruled out in the way by which the leader exercises Christian authority. Outward force can produce conformity, but it can

139

never produce that inner commitment which moves persons to choose to follow Jesus.

How, then, does the servant lead? By serving! The secular ruler speaks his commands, but the spiritual leader demonstrates by his example the Kingdom way of life into which he is called to lead others. No wonder Peter picked up this same theme and wrote, as an elder to fellow elders, "Be shepherds of God's flock that is under your care . . . not lording it over those entrusted to you, but being examples to the flock" (I Pet. 5:2, 3). By serving, the Christian leader demonstrates the greatness of the love of God and gently motivates others to follow Him. "Whoever wants to be first must be your slave—just as the Son of Man did not come to be served, but to serve, and to give his life a ransom for many" (Mt. 20:27, 28).

A LAST EXAMPLE

Matthew 20:29-34

The disciples had asked about greatness in Jesus' present Kingdom. Jesus had answered them—fully. Greatness involves humbling ourselves and taking our place as one of God's little ones. Greatness involves accepting others as little ones, too: seeking to restore them when they go astray, having patience, and always being willing to let forgiveness wash away the hurts that sin must bring. Greatness also involves rejecting the attractive but destructive ways in which religious people often

140

seek greatness. Legalism, good deeds, hard work—none of these can produce greatness in Christ's Kingdom.

Finally, Jesus has given us His own clear prescription for greatness. Learn how to lead others *as a servant*. Be one of those men or women who choose to drink Jesus' cup and give up their lives for the sake of others.

Then Matthew recorded a deeply moving incident that helps us see what Jesus' kind of greatness is. As they were going through Jericho, a great crowd followed Jesus. Two blind men, sitting by the road, heard that Jesus was passing by. They cried out to Him. The crowd callously told them to shut up. But the two only called louder.

And Jesus stopped.

He was on His way to Jerusalem, toward His trial and Crucifixion. He was burdened by great crowds who did not care and disciples who did not understand. But Jesus set aside His own burdens and needs at this call for help. The Bible says, "Jesus had compassion on them and touched their eyes. Immediately they received their sight and followed him" (20:34).

Jesus stopped—for the individual in the crowd.

Jesus cared—for the outcasts whom the crowd considered to be worthless.

This is greatness. To touch in compassion, and to give ourselves to others as their servant for Jesus' sake, is the one way that we, too, can lead.

Let's let God's Word throw off *our* blindness and, following Jesus, become great.

141

GOING DEEPER

to personalize

1. For *one* of the following passages, (a) describe the kind of person who most needs this teaching, and (b) describe how it will help him.

Matthew 18   Matthew 20:1-6
Matthew 19   Matthew 20:17-34

2. The text develops three contrasts between the secular ruler and servant leaders presented by Jesus in Matthew 20:17-28. List as many additonal comparisons and contrasts as you can.

3. From your study of Matthew 20:17-28 (above), write a two-page paper on the nature of Christian leadership.

4. In what ways are *you* called to be a leader?

to probe

"Authority" is something greatly misunderstood in Christian as well as secular worlds today. Go beyond what is seen in the Matthew 10 and Matthew 20 passages and, using the whole of the New Testament, write a paper showing how you understand "authority" in the Church.

CONFRONTATION

WE HAVE A TENDENCY TODAY to see gentleness as weakness.

This tendency probably explains, at least partially, why people of all times tend to draw back from Jesus' picture of leadership as servanthood. "But," they object, "we want leaders who are *strong*. We want leaders with authority." The fact of the matter is that only in Christ's kind of servanthood do we find true spiritual strength. Gentleness is *not* weakness. Compassion is becoming to the King.

So it is not Mr. Milquetoast that Jesus sets before us as our example, but Himself. In these next chapters, which portray Jesus in direct conflict with His enemies, we see Him speak out boldly in His full authority as King. In dealing with little ones the leader is gentle. In facing foes he is bold.

THE TRIUMPHAL ENTRY

Matthew 21:1-17

It was the Passover week, a few brief days before the Crucifixion. Coming to Jerusalem, Jesus sent two of His disciples to bring a donkey and colt to Him for a long-prophesied entry into Jerusalem. Isaiah and Zechariah had both spoken of it:

> Your king comes to you,
> gentle and riding on a donkey,
> on a colt, the foal of a donkey.
>
> *Matthew 21:5*

Without pomp, humble and on a humble beast of burden, the King would come.

On this day the crowds that soon would turn against Jesus swelled with enthusiasm for Him. "Hosanna to the Son of David!" they shouted. "Blessed is he who comes in the name of the Lord!" (21:9).

Christ moved purposefully to the Temple. There He went into the court, which was to be reserved for prayer, and found merchants.

The Old Testament ruled that only unblemished animals might be offered in sacrifice. The priests set up a very lucrative trade in "approved" lambs and pigeons. Animals brought from the country for sacrifice could easily be disapproved by priestly inspectors, and worshipers forced to buy from the Temple merchants. What had been set aside for prayer had become a "den of robbers" (21:13)!

144

As Jesus stood in the cleansed Temple yard, the blind and the lame came to Him and He healed them. With even greater enthusiasm the crowds proclaimed, "Hosanna to the Son of David!" The chief priests and scribes saw all these wonderful things which Jesus did and "they were indignant" (21:15). Hardened as ever, they were totally unwilling to recognize Jesus as their King.

THE EMPTINESS OF LEGALISM

Matthew 21:18–22:14

When evening fell, Jesus and his companions went across the valley to Bethany for the night. The next morning an incident occurred which gives us the key to the significance of the events which followed.

On the way back to Jerusalem, Jesus saw a fig tree and went over to it, as if to pluck some of its fruit for breakfast. Although the foliage was luxuriant, there was no fruit. Jesus uttered a curse, and "immediately the tree withered" (21:19). Impressed, the disciples asked, How did the fig tree wither so quickly?" (21:20). Jesus' explanation was simple: "Faith."

The fig tree of Israel which *appeared* luxuriant had produced no fruit. It was to wither away, its fruitlessness to be exposed. Faith was to provide a better way. Immediately upon entering the city, Jesus began a series of confrontations and teachings which reveal why the legalism of the Jewish

145

leaders, like the hypocritical fig tree, produced only appearance rather than fruit.

Empty of authority (Mt. 21:23-27). In Deuteronomy, the Jewish people were told to take disputes to their rulers for them to settle. The elders of the people challenged Jesus and asked by what authority He was acting. Christ asked them a question: "John's baptism—where did it come from? Was it from heaven, or from men?" The elders were thrown into confusion. If they said "from heaven," Jesus would condemn them for not listening. But if they said "from men," the crowds who held that John was a prophet may even have attacked them! Unwilling and unable to exercise the authority they claimed, they replied "We don't know" (21:27).

Untouched by changed lives (Mt. 21:28-32). Jesus then told a parable, which He explained. The leaders were like a son who professes obedience but in practice will not do what his father has asked. Even when they had seen open sinners respond and change their ways (the disobedient son in the parable who later repented and chose to do his father's will), still the leaders did not respond. They were untouched by the evidence of transformed lives, for they did not, in fact, care about people or about their relationship with God.

The desire for personal power (Mt. 21:33-46). What then *did* the leaders care about? Jesus launched into another parable, about an owner who leased his vineyards to tenants. They were to care for it and then give the owner his share of the profit. When

146

messengers were sent to the tenants, they beat and stoned and killed them. Finally the owner sent his own son. The tenants' reaction? "Come, let's kill him and *take his inheritance*" (21:38).

Again the parable was devastatingly clear. The Old Testament speaks often of Israel as God's vineyard (cf. Isa. 5:1-7). The servants God sent were the prophets, which earlier generations had rejected and often killed. Now, in Jesus, the Son had come. And the reaction of the rulers had been to plot to kill Him!

The Jewish leaders might speak of their pure and holy reverence for God and His Law. But, in fact, their motive was one of pride and a lust for power that would not permit them to take their place with God's other little ones.

And so Jesus pronounced judgment. "I tell you that the kingdom of God will be taken away from you and given to a people who will produce its fruit" (Mt. 21:43).

Pretensions withered (Mt. 22:1-14). Before this scornful expose, all the pretentions of the Pharisees are withered, just as the leaves of the fig tree. Looking ahead to the day when He will come into His Kingdom, and using the common picture of the marriage feast (cf. Rev. 19:7), Jesus proclaimed that those who have been invited and have refused to come will be replaced by others, both bad and good, who will respond to the King's call. As was the custom, those coming are to be provided with a wedding garment by the Father in exchange for their own. Anyone seeking to crash the feast will be

147

recognized immediately; his own covering will not be acceptable. And he will be cast "into the darkness" (22:13).

The exposure of the rulers is complete.

COUNTERATTACK

Matthew 22:15-46

Desperate then, and afraid of the reaction of the people if they took direct action against Jesus (21:46), the rulers determined to entangle Jesus in His talk.

The Pharisees (22:15-22). The strength of the Pharisees was their complete commitment to the Law and their rejection of all that was Gentile and foreign. The Greek culture which influenced the Sadducee party was totally rejected by the Pharisees, who had a reputation with the people of standing firm for Jewish ways. So a delegation of Pharisees approached Jesus, hoping to trap Him.

"Tell us then," they asked. "Is it right to pay taxes to Caesar or not?" (22:17).

They must have been very pleased with this trap. If Jesus directed them *not* to pay taxes, the Roman overseers could be informed and might take action. If Jesus said they *should* pay taxes, the Pharisees were sure He would lose popularity with the people. The insult of paying taxes to Rome through tax collectors, who normally took two or three times what was due, uniquely roused the hostility of the Jews.

148

Jesus asked His enemies for a coin. When the Pharisees brought it to Him, He asked them whose inscription and picture it bore. "Caesar's," the Pharisees said. "Give to Caesar what is Caesar's," Jesus responded, "and to God what is God's" (22:21). Stunned, the Pharisees left Him and went away.

The Sadducees (Mt. 22:23-33). Sadducees have been mentioned earlier in Matthew, but we have not yet introduced them. For about a hundred years, the Sadducees and Pharisees were competing parties in Palestine. The word Sadducee seems to come from a root meaning "judge." They were, however, an aristocracy, which controlled the high priesthood and thus gained political power.

Like many an aristocracy, they were exclusive and proud. Theologically they were liberals who rejected the oral law exalted by the Pharisees, and who also rejected such doctrines as that of resurrection and angels. They were the kind of people who were tempted to adjust their views to the "modern" notions of the educated men of their world.

Although in conflict with the Pharisees, the Sadducees had to accommodate themselves to them because of the Pharisees' influence over the masses. But when Jesus appeared, these traditional enemies quickly arrived at a truce. Their mutual hatred and fear of the King brought them together.

Now the Sadducees raised one of those hypothetical questions with which they had long taunted those who held the position of the Pharisees on

149

resurrection. They spoke of a woman who had been successively married to seven brothers. "At the resurrection, whose wife will she be . . . ?" (22:28), the Sadducees asked. Jesus' response was a rebuke, pointing out that these proud men were strangers both to the Scriptures and to God's power. In the resurrection, people will not marry. And as far as resurrection is concerned, the Scriptures reveal God as one who *is* (not *was!*) the God of Abraham, Isaac, and Jacob. God is God not of the dead, but of the living.

The lawyer (Mt. 22:34-45). Once again the Pharisee party attempted to trap Jesus. This time a lawyer (one who was an expert in the oral and written Law) asked Jesus to name the first and greatest commandment. Answering, Jesus then asked the Pharisees a question in return.

"What do you think about the Christ [Messiah]? Whose son is he?" (22:42). The Pharisees answered correctly: "David's." Then Jesus asked, "How is it then that David, speaking by the Spirit, calls him Lord?" (22:43).

The point is, of course, that no human father calls his son Lord, for in the culture of the Middle East the son always owed deference and respect to his father. The only explanation had to be that David's Descendant is more than human. He is, in fact, as the Old Testament itself foretells, the Son of God.

The Pharisees were unable to answer a single word. They went away, and no one dared to challenge Jesus to debate again.

THE SCRIBES AND PHARISEES DENOUNCED

Matthew 23

Then, in one of the most scathing indictments imaginable, Jesus cataloged the faults of the Pharisees—faults of which all of us must be wary, and particularly those who stand in places of spiritual leadership.

They preached, but did not practice (23:3).

They acted only to be seen and admired by other men (23:5).

They were proud, seeking to be prominent and to be exalted over other men (23:6-9). Rejecting humility and servanthood, they themselves were rejected by God (23:10-12).

They were hypocrites who neither responded to God nor let others respond (23:13-15).

They were blind guides who played with man-made rules and missed the great realities (23:16-22).

They were hypocrites who made a great to-do over strict tithing of the leaves of tiny herbs like mint and dill, but neglected great matters like justice and mercy (23:23-24).

They were hypocrites who focused on outward appearances when within they were filled with greed and pride (23:25-27).

They were just like their fathers (predecessors) who, when they had authority, killed the prophets and the wise men God sent to Israel. In that generation's rejection of Jesus, the blood guilt of the ages was coming to rest on them (23:28-36).

Against the background of this indictment, we are given one last touching portrait as Jesus spoke His last words to the men who had opposed Him—and to the crowds who would soon scream for His death.

O Jerusalem, Jerusalem, you who kill the prophets and stone those sent to you, how often I have longed to gather your children together, as a hen gathers her chicks under her wings, but you were not willing. Look, your house is left to you desolate. For I tell you, you will not see me again until you say, Blessed is he who comes in the name of the Lord.

Matthew 23:37-39

GOING DEEPER

to personalize

1. When do you think Christians have the right or obligation to be bold in confronting others as Jesus did here?

2. Some of Jesus' parables are designed to make a single point, while others are designed to give many points of comparison. Examine the parable of the wedding feast (Mt. 22:1-14), and jot down *all* the points you think Jesus seems to be making.

3. From Matthew 23, develop a set of ten posi . tive commandments for Christian leaders. (Note that the very points at which the Pharisees are condemned can be reversed to give positive guidelines.)

4. Which of the positive commandments you developed seem most important for you personally to follow, and why?

to probe

1. The following references from the Old Testament are related in some way to Matthew 21:1-17. Study them, and write a brief paper on the significance of this passage in view of Old Testament prophecy.

Zechariah 9:9; II Kings 9:13; Psalm 118:26; Exodus 30:13; Leviticus 1:14; Isaiah 56:7; Jeremiah 7:11; Psalm 8:2.

2. A prophecy in Daniel 9 (specifically vs. 25) gives a definite time that "Messiah the Prince" will come, as measured from the decree by a pagan king to rebuild Jerusalem after the Babylonian Captivity. Sir Robert Anderson, in a classic book called *The Coming Prince,* has demonstrated that Jesus' entry into Jerusalem as recorded in this passage fulfilled the prophecy *to the day.* Skim this book to gain a special appreciation for the accuracy and trustworthiness of Bible prophecy.

THE FUTURE
OF THE KINGDOM

MANY PEOPLE have enjoyed playing games with the Bible, raising all sorts of objections and pointing out all sorts of supposed errors. The foolish raise silly objections that can be easily answered: Where did Cain get his wife? Doesn't the Bible say the earth is flat? How can you believe the Bible since it talks about the sun going around the earth?

This kind of surface and superficial thing is easily explained, particularly as the queries are obviously raised by people who know nothing about the Bible. Any serious student of Scripture can raise far more basic and difficult issues. Without doubt, one of the most difficult for many is this: What happened to the prophesied Old Testament Kingdom? If God did not keep His word about establishing that Kingdom, how can we trust anything in the Word?

This question troubled the disciples. Jesus told them He was approaching a Cross, not a crown.

They could not grasp what was happening. They were sure God's Word is trustworthy, but not at all sure how He would keep His promises if He, the King, were to die.

This concern of the twelve surfaced as Jesus led them away from the Temple after announcing judgment on the Pharisees. Glancing at the towering Temple building, Jesus remarked that each stone of the Temple would be thrown down, and "not one stone here will be left on another" (24:2). This destruction was accomplished four decades later in A.D. 70 by a Roman army under Titus, a general who would later become emperor.

That evening the disciples came to ask Jesus about the future, about that time when Christ would come again and the age would close. In answering them, Jesus gives us our answers as well.

THE FUTURE

The Bible speaks a great deal in both Old and New Testaments about the future. Some "prophecy" in both Testaments involves forthtelling: communicating a message from God. But most prophecy involves foretelling which involves telling what will happen *before the historical events occur.*

Foretelling may involve either near events or events that are far distant to the prophet's day. Thus, Jeremiah spoke both of the death of a false prophet, Hananiah (Jer. 28), to take place within one year, and of a New Covenant to be made with the house of Israel which was actually ratified hundreds of years later by Christ at Calvary (Jer. 32).

Prophecy's purpose. What is important to note, however, is that in prophecy the *time elements and sequences* are seldom clear. This is Peter's point in I Peter 1:10, 11, when he notes that the prophets themselves puzzled over "the time and circumstances" the Spirit who inspired their words intended. The prophets had insights into the foretold events, but they could not fit them together.

This is a very important thing to remember when we study prophecy. We do not really know the time when prophesied events will happen, or even the exact sequences. Thus, it is always dangerous to attempt to erect tight prophetic systems in which we confidently sequence the future according to clues provided in the Word. Prophecy is not designed to give us a "future history book" which can be written before the events. While we do know the broad outlines of the future from Scripture, we can never be too sure about the systems we construct from them.

As a matter of fact, an approach to prophetic studies which majors on constructing systems misses something basic about Bible prophecy. Bible prophecy is meant to have an impact on the present. Prophecy is designed to have a penetrating impact on our lives and values now. Thus, when Peter speaks of the fact that our present universe will one day be dissolved in a fervent heat, he does so to challenge values: "Seeing then that all these things shall be dissolved, what manner of men ought ye to be" (II Pet. 3:11, KJV). When Paul

157

speaks so beautifully of the rapture in Thessalonians, it is not so that you and I might argue over whether it comes in the middle or at the beginning of the Tribulation. It is so that we might "encourage each other" (I Thess. 4:18) with the realization that when Jesus comes, all believers will be together with Him. The dead we mourn will be our eternal companions. When John speaks of Jesus' return it is not to locate it in relation to Daniel's seventieth week, but to help us realize that "when he shall appear, we shall be like him; for we shall see him as he is" (I Jn. 3:2, 3, KJV).

Thus, when we come to a study of the future in any part of our Bible we want to be careful to resist the temptation to speculate on details, and instead seek to discern the major emphasis of the passage. We need to keep the *purpose* of the prophetic passage in clear view.

Relationship between Old Testament and New Testament prophecy. When looking at New Testament prophecy, and particularly at prophetic segments of the Gospels, it is important to be very clear about the relationship between events foretold in the two Testaments.

First, we need to remember that there is full harmony between the Old Testament and the New in prophecy, as in all things. The New Testament does not replace the Old. Thus, we have Christ's own affirmation in Matthew's Gospel that the Kingdom expected on the basis of the Old Testament *will* come. "I tell you the truth, at the renewal of all things, when the Son of Man sits on his throne

158

in heavenly glory, you who have followed me will also sit on twelve thrones, judging the twelve tribes of Israel" (19:28). Matthew 24:15 confirms that the future foretold by Daniel and associated with setting up the "everlasting Kingdom" will come to pass. There is no doubt that Jesus expected, and promised, a time "when the Son of Man comes in his glory, and all the angels with him, he will sit on his throne in heavenly glory." (25:31).

The glorious Kingdom of the Old Testament, expected by Israel and by the disciples themselves, *will surely come.*

Second, since the New Testament does not supersede or replace the Old, we can accept the broad outline of the future developed in the Old Testament as the basic framework within which to understand the teachings of the New. God has not gone back on His word. Instead, he has demonstrated a greater complexity and variety to His eternal plans and purposes than were earlier revealed.

The basic pattern of God's prophetic plan for the future is explored in *Springtime Coming,* the fifth book of the Old Testament series of these studies. In general, the broad outlines of the "time of the end" given in the Old Testament feature:

- nations of the earth divided in western, northern, and eastern power blocks
- the western power block headed by the Anti-Christ
- increasing tension over the Middle East, lead-

ing to a treaty in which the western powers
guarantee the integrity of the Jewish state
- increasing worldwide troubles and disasters,
  gradually intensifying
- tremendous tribulation for Israel, involving
  persecution by the western powers and finally
  invasion and desolation by the northern
- personal coming and intervention of Christ,
  the Messiah, who will defeat Israel's enemies
  and set up a righteous Kingdom of worldwide
  extent.

It is helpful as we read Christ's portrait of the
future in Matthew to remember this outline, and to
notice that Jesus is clearly talking within that Old
Testament framework!

Third, we want to note that the New Testament
provides not a revision of God's plan but rather an
addition to it. This, of course, is the point of Jesus'
quote of Psalm 78:2 in Matthew 13:35: "I will utter
things hidden since the creation of the world." This
is also what Paul is referring to in Colossians where
he speaks of himself as a minister charged with
making fully known "the mystery that has been
kept hidden for ages and generations, but is now
disclosed to the saints" (1:26).

In short, then, the answer to the question of
"What happened to the Kingdom?" is "Nothing!" It
is still to come.

The Old Testament speaks of both a suffering
and a reigning Messiah, but makes no clear time
distinctions. The whole intervening age between

the Messiah's Resurrection and return is not a subject of Old Testament prophecy, but a new dimension of God's eternal plan introduced by Jesus during His lifetime as the "unexpected form of the Kingdom." It is the Age of the Church.

With this background, we can go back to look at Matthew 24 and 25. We realize immediately that the questions which stimulated this discourse were asked from an Old Testament frame of reference and are answered in that frame of reference. Matthew 24 and 25 are, in fact, Jesus' affirmation that the glorious Kingdom which Israel expected will surely come. If we understand the content of Old Testament prophecy, we have no doubts about the meaning and impact of Jesus' words here.

JESUS' WORDS OF PROPHECY

Matthew 24, 25

These chapters contain Jesus' answers to three questions posed by His disciples. "Tell us," they asked, "[1] when will this happen, and [2] what will be the sign of your coming and [3] of the end of the age?" (24:3). The questions were answered—but in reverse order.

Signs of the end of the age (Mt. 24:4-26). The picture given in this section of Matthew 24 is of a time of increasing tension, disaster, and disturbance. Wars and rumors of wars, earthquakes, increasing wickedness, and persecution of Jesus' followers are all involved.

None of these is in itself that striking; there have

161

always been wars, and earthquakes often dot the news with tragedy. But there are aspects of this picture which make it the description of a unique time which is the subject of much Old Testament prophecy.

- The common disasters were identified by Jesus as "the beginning of birth pains" (24:8).
- Events Jesus spoke of are identified in the Old Testament Book of Daniel as taking place in the seven-year period just before the Messiah will establish His earthly Kingdom (24:15).
- The Tribulation which is said to come then will be a "great distress, unequaled from the beginning of the world until now—and never to be equaled again" (24:21).

In the Old Testament this time of worldwide trouble is given various names: "the time of Jacob's trouble," "that day," "the day of the Lord," and "the tribulation." Against this Old Testament background, the disciples would quickly identify the time of which Jesus spoke!

What will be the sign of your coming? (Mt. 24:27-31). Jesus' answer to this question was far less specific. There is, in fact, no single "sign" identified. Yet, several striking aspects of Jesus' return are given.

First, Jesus' coming will be visible, seen as clearly as spectacular lightning from horizon to horizon (24:27). Christ's coming will follow immediately after the Tribulation and will be accompanied by great and dramatic physical disturbances in the heavens. There will be an unidentified "sign" in the heavens, with deep mourning as the Son is seen to return in power and great glory (24:30). Jesus' coming will initiate an angelic regathering of His elect (for this Old Testament context, cf. Isa. 27:13; Zech. 9:14).

Nothing more is told. But how great a contrast between Jesus' return and His first coming. Then He came in lowliness, a King, humbling Himself to be a servant, unrecognized and rejected by men. When He returns it will be in power and might and glory to rule.

When will this be? (Mt. 24:32–25:46). Jesus answered this third question exhaustively. But only after saying, "No one knows about that day or hour, not even the angels in heaven, nor the Son, but only the Father" (24:36).

Nevertheless, it is this question Jesus chose to explore in greatest depth. It is the answer to this question which has the most significance for the disciples and for us.

This generation will certainly not pass away (Mt. 24:32-35). The Tribulation events previously described are like buds on a tree before the leaves come. The bud is evidence that the time of flowering is near. But one thing Jesus promised: "This generation will certainly not pass away" (24:34) till all He has spoken of comes to pass.

What "generation" is Jesus speaking of? The term used here does not indicate people alive at that day, but Israel as a race. (Some interpret it to mean the living generation actually undergoing the

163

Tribulation time.) By either interpretation, this was Jesus' promise of preservation. The time of trouble will not be the end of the Jewish people or of mankind.

What then did Jesus say about the time of His coming, and the time *until* His coming?

Watch for His coming (Mt. 24:36-44). As in Noah's day, before the Flood swept everything away, the people living in the day just before Jesus returns will be involved in their own affairs, blind to the significance of the happenings around them.

Because the day when the Son will come is unexpected, we are to "watch." "So," Jesus said, "you also must be ready, because the Son of Man will come at an hour when you do not expect him."

Responsible servants (Mt. 24:45-51). What is to be done by servants who are looking for their lord's return? They are to remember they have been given responsibility for their master's household.

The danger Jesus warned against is a real one. He said, "But suppose that servant is wicked and says to himself, 'My master is staying away a long time. . . . The master . . . will come . . . when he does not expect him" (24:48-50). Faithfulness involves taking proper care of God's household, knowing that the Lord will appear at an unexpected time.

The ten maidens (Mt. 25:1-13). This is the well-known story of the ten maidens who took lamps and went to meet the bridegroom who was coming for his bride. Unprepared for a long wait, five ran out of oil when the bridegroom was delayed.

Again, Jesus warned, "Watch, because you do not know the day or the hour" (25:13).

The talents (Mt. 25:14-30). The parable of the talents again emphasizes the same elements. A lord leaves on a journey, making his servants responsible for his possessions. While he is away, the servants are to use the gifts they have been given for the benefit of their master. One day the master will return, and then there will be an accounting.

Each of these stories drives home an important point: What God has promised will come to pass. But our time is not to be spent dreaming of that future day. It is to be spent in the service of our absent Lord who has entrusted His possession to us. Christ the King has entrusted to us this unexpected and unprophesied form of His Kingdom!

Being ready for His coming means being involved as servants in the ongoing ministries committed to us by our Lord.

THE GATHERING OF THE NATIONS

Matthew 25:31-46

Then Jesus turned again to His Second Coming. "When the Son of Man comes in his glory, and all the angels with him, he will sit on his throne in heavenly glory" (v. 31). Christ went on to discuss the ministry of judgment He will undertake at that day. Again in the Old Testament, roots of the picture He sketched are clear. Christ looked ahead to describe a prophesied time when all the nations on the earth will be gathered before Him.

FIGURE VI   MATTHEW'S TEACHING ON THE KINGDOM

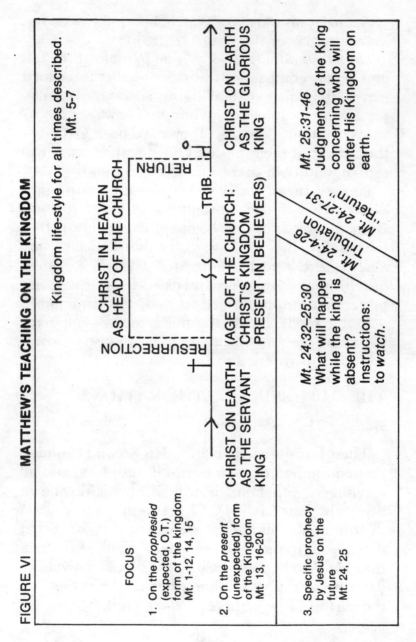

Kingdom life-style for all times described.
Mt. 5-7

CHRIST IN HEAVEN
AS HEAD OF THE CHURCH

RESURRECTION   RETURN

TRIB.

(AGE OF THE CHURCH:
CHRIST'S KINGDOM
PRESENT IN BELIEVERS)

CHRIST ON EARTH
AS THE SERVANT
KING

CHRIST ON EARTH
AS THE GLORIOUS
KING

FOCUS

1. On the *prophesied*
   (expected, O.T.)
   form of the kingdom
   Mt. 1-12, 14, 15

2. On the *present*
   (unexpected) form
   of the Kingdom
   Mt. 13, 16-20

3. Specific prophecy
   by Jesus on the
   future
   Mt. 24, 25

Mt. 24:32–25:30
What will happen
while the king is
absent?
Instructions:
to watch.

Mt. 24:4-26
Tribulation

Mt. 24:27-31
"Return"

Mt. 25:31-46
Judgments of the King
concerning who will
enter His Kingdom on
earth.

The peoples of the world will be separated into two groups, one destined to enter the Kingdom over which the Messiah will rule. The term "nations" here does not refer to national groups but to the Gentile world in contrast to "brothers of mine," brothers who have been naked, hungry, thirsty, imprisoned and sick. The Jewish brothers will have undergone a great Tribulation—and will have been restored to faith in the Messiah they once rejected.

This is a picture not of man's final judgment but, as the text indicates, judgment on a generation of men living at the time of Jesus' coming. The prize is not eternal life but inheritance of the Kingdom prepared for Gentiles as well as for believing Israel (25:34).

The Old Testament picture of the future is *not* wrong, for the promised Kingdom will come when the King returns. And we can leave the details of that time to God.

There is for us a different focus for our lives. We expect His return, and so we wholeheartedly serve Him. We minister as servants in a household which He has left with us until He comes to take up His throne.

GOING DEEPER

to personalize

1. One of the basic questions in Biblical interpretations is this: Has the Church replaced Israel in God's plans? For added insight into this question,

read Paul's answer in Romans 11 (noting particularly vss. 25-27 in the argument).

2. It is very clear that most of this section of Matthew concerns a time when the King is absent, Jesus focuses our attention on what will be happening during this time. The emphasis in this specific "while away" segment (Mt. 24:32—25:30) is application: instructions for us, the King's servants. Study this section, and explain the implications of these common elements for our lives today.

- the key figure absent
- an uncertain time of return
- responsibility for the absentee's possessions
- emphasis on watching
- evaluation of behavior while the key figure is gone

3. Does the aspect of punishment here indicate that believers can be "lost"? Why do you think it is here? What is Christ teaching us?

to probe

Find three Old Testament passages (not isolated verses) that parallel Jesus' teaching about the Great Tribulation. From them describe the Old Testament perspective.

THE FINAL TRIAL

IF JESUS' PROPHETIC PICTURE of the Kingdom's future has its roots in the Old Testament, what is about to happen has even deeper roots. All of revelation focuses on the events of these next few days: millennia and centuries of time strain forward to it, while additional millennia and centuries find meaning by looking back to it.

Matthew puts it in perspective as he gives us Jesus' words, "As you know, the Passover is two days away" (26:2).

Passover. The Passover was the time of beginning for Israel. Passover marked the new year; the Passover month was the beginning of months. The annual Passover festival recalled a particular event through which God had won for Israel freedom from bondage in Egypt and independence as a nation.

Exodus 11 and 12 record the story. Great

plagues ruined the land of Egypt but failed to move Egypt's ruler to let the slave race, Israel, go. God determined a final judgment. In preparation, each Hebrew family was to select a lamb. For four days, the lamb was to be kept in the home; then on the fourth day it was to be killed. That evening the blood of the lamb was sprinkled on the doorposts and lintel of each Jewish home, and the lamb itself roasted and eaten. That very night, God's death angel passed through the land of Egypt and killed the firstborn son of every home. But he passed over those homes protected by the blood.

Each year following, the Jews were commanded by God to commemorate those events by reenactment. The lambs were slain, the blood sprinkled, and each generation was retaught the lesson that freedom could come only through the shedding of the blood of the lamb.

The Passover. Jesus was about to fulfill the deepest meaning of that Old Testament rite. Passover not only looked back to the Exodus; it also looked forward to the Cross. "The Passover is two days away," Jesus said, "and the Son of Man will be handed over to be crucified" (26:2).

John the Baptist had foreseen it that day back at the river Jordan. "Look, the Lamb of God," he had said, "who takes away the sin of the world!" (Jn. 1:29). For three to four more years Jesus had been among the Jewish people, teaching, healing, caring. But when the Passover came, like the Lamb He was, He, too, had to die—that through His death His people might find the ultimate freedom: freedom

170

from sin and sin's power—freedom from the fear of death.

The culminating act of service and self-giving had been clearly taught in the Old Testament, even apart from the Passover symbolism. We see it, for instance, in Isaiah 53. The death of Christ and its meaning are so clear that as we read this passage we can hardly believe we are reading words penned over 600 years before Jesus' birth.

He grew up before him like a young plant,
    and like a root out of dry ground;
he had no form or comeliness that
    we should look at him,
and no beauty that we should desire him.
He was despised and rejected by men;
    a man of sorrows, and acquainted with grief;
and as one from whom men hide their faces
    he was despised, and we esteemed him not.

Surely he had borne our griefs
    and carried our sorrows;
yet we esteemed him stricken,
    smitten by God, and afflicted.
But he was wounded for our transgressions,
    he was bruised for our iniquities;
upon him was the chastisement that made us
        whole,
    and with his stripes we are healed.
All we like sheep have gone astray;
    we have turned every one to his own way;
and the Lord has laid on him
    the iniquity of us all.

He was oppressed, and he was afflicted,
   yet he opened not his mouth;
like a lamb that is led to the slaughter,
   and like a sheep that before its shearers is
     dumb,
   so he opened not his mouth.
By oppression and judgment he was taken away;
   and as for his generation, who considered
that he was cut off out of the land
   of the living,
   stricken for the transgression of my people?

And they made his grave with the wicked
   and with a rich man in his death,
although he had done no violence,
   and there was no deceit in his mouth.

Yet it was the will of the Lord to bruise him;
   he has put him to grief;
when he makes himself an offering for sin,
   he shall see his offspring, he shall
   prolong his days;
the will of the Lord shall prosper in his hand;
   he shall see the fruit of the travail of his
   soul and be satisfied;
by his knowledge shall the righteous one,
   my servant,
   make many to be accounted righteous,
   and he shall bear their iniquities.
Therefore I will divide him a portion with the
     great,
   and he shall divide the spoil with the strong;
   because he poured out his soul to death,

and was numbered with the transgressors;
yet he bore the sin of many,
and made intercession for the transgressors.

Isaiah 53:2-12, (RSV)

THE LAST DAYS

Matthew 26, 27

The culminating events then occurred with tragic swiftness. Jesus was anointed with expensive ointment, an act symbolic of preparation for burial (26:6-13). Judas slipped away to make an arrangement with the chief priests to betray Jesus to them when the crowds were not present. He settled on a price: 30 pieces of silver (26:14-16).

When morning came, Jesus sent His disciples to arrange a hall where they would eat the Passover meal together (26:17-19). That night, after the meal and before the discourse recorded in John 13-16, Judas left again to finalize plans to take Jesus prisoner (26:20-29).

On the way out of Jerusalem, Jesus told the disciples that they would all flee and leave Him to face His fate alone. Peter boldly led a chorus of objections; they would all die with Him first (26:30-35). Arriving at a garden called Gethsemane, Jesus asked His disciples to wait as He went aside to pray. This deeply moving prayer in which Christ shared the sense of burden and agony He felt in approaching the Cross is recorded for us (26:36-39). But the disciples were too tired to be moved; they drifted off to sleep. Christ, sensing the utter loneliness of the condemned, urged them to stay awake to watch with Him. But again they dozed off as Christ returned to prayer (26:40-46).

Then the light of flickering torches was seen, and the sounds of an armed mob heard. Led by Judas, the mob hung back as he advanced to identify Jesus with a kiss (26:45-50). Immediately the crowd surged forward, and servants of the priests roughly pinned Jesus' arms behind Him. Peter boldly drew a sword and struck out! "Put it away," Jesus told him. If Christ had intended to resist, angel armies could have been summoned. "But how then would the Scriptures be fulfilled that say it must happen in this way?" (26:54). When Jesus turned to face the mob, the disciples scattered (26:51-56).

Then began the long night of trial. Jesus was taken to the high priest's home where the council was gathered to try Him at night (an illegal act by Jewish Law). Their witnesses were brought to charge Him, but even their lies could not raise a charge meriting death. Finally the high priest asked Jesus directly: "Tell us if you are the Christ, the Son of God" (26:63). Christ's response was both an admission and affirmation: "Yes, it is as you say. But I say to all of you: In the future you will see the Son of Man sitting at the right hand of the Mighty One, and coming on the clouds of heaven" (26:64). At this the high priest cried, "Blasphemy!" And blasphemy is a crime for which the Old Testament prescribes death (26:57-65)! The court then passed judgment: "He is worthy of death" (26:66). Immediately they began to treat Jesus as a convicted

174

criminal, slapping and spitting on Him and mocking (26:66-68).

Meanwhile Peter was sitting outside the house where all this was taking place. He had run, but he still had the courage to follow. Yet, when he was confronted by a serving maid and then by other bystanders and charged with being one of Jesus' followers, Peter denied it with a curse! A cock crowed, and Peter remembered that when Jesus told the disciples they would scatter He also told Peter that he would deny Him three times before morning. Sobbing uncontrollably, Peter stumbled away into the dawn (26:69-75).

Back inside, the rulers of the Jews had a problem. The Romans ruled in Palestine, and while a measure of self-government was granted to the Jews, they did not have the authority to execute anyone. So they packed Jesus off to Pilate, the Roman governor (27:1-2).

Meanwhile, Judas had discovered that Christ had actually been condemned to death. Hurrying back to the Temple priests, he returned the 30 pieces of silver and cried out, "I have sinned, for I have betrayed innocent blood" (27:4). Unmoved, these men whose office made them mediators between repentant sinners and God, coldly replied, "What is that to us? That's your responsibility" (27:4). Throwing down the money, Judas rushed out—and hanged himself. And the priests—ever careful to "obey" the Law whose spirit and intent they daily distorted—argued over the blood money which it was not "lawful" to put back into the Temple treas-

175

ury. Finally, they used it to buy a burial ground for indigents (27:3-10).

Jesus then stood before the Roman governor, and there admitted that He is King of the Jews. Beyond this, He refused to defend Himself against the attack of the chief priests and elders (27:11-14).

Pilate was clearly unhappy with the situation. Even while sitting on the judgment seat, a messenger from his wife arrived, speaking of a dream she had had, and warning Pilate to have nothing to do with "that innocent man" (27:19). Squirming, Pilate offered the crowd, which had by then gathered, a choice. He would release Jesus or Barabbas, a murderer who was also sentenced to death. Persuaded by their leaders, the very people who a few days before shouted out "Hosanna," now were screaming, "Crucify him!" (27:22). Pilate tried to reason with the mob. But their only response was a swelling chant, repeating over and over with bestial rhythm, "Crucify him!"

Overwhelmed by the passion of the mob, Pilate feared a riot. Already unpopular with the Jews, he did not wish to risk a charge of supporting one who claimed to be a King! Washing his hands, Pilate announced the words that permitted Jesus' execution. Quickly the Jews accepted the implications of Pilate's symbolic washing of his hands: "His blood be on us and on our children!" (27:25). Releasing Barabbas, Pilate turned Jesus over to the soldiers to be beaten and mocked in preparation for His execution (27:24-31).

Later, on the way outside the city to the execution hill, Jesus stumbled and fell under the weight of His cross. A visitor to the city, Simon, was pulled from the crowd by the soldiers and made to carry it for Him. At the place of execution called Golgotha, a sign was nailed to the wooden stake, reading, "THIS IS JESUS, THE KING OF THE JEWS" (27:37). When all was ready, Jesus refused a drugged drink designed to lessen the pain. Prostrate on the wooden post, spikes were driven through His living flesh. Then, with a tearing jolt, the pole was lifted—hung poised—and dropped into the hole prepared to receive it.

Jesus, King of the Jews, hung outlined against the sky, flanked by two dying criminals.

Jesus, who walked the lanes of Palestine to heal the sick, and feed the hungry, and free men and women tormented in the grip of demons, was hanging in suspended agony as passersby paused to watch—and ridicule (27:32-44).

Suddenly, about noon, a stunning darkness blotted out the sun. A hush fell. Near three in the afternoon the figure on the cross convulsed, and cried out: "My God, my God, why have you forsaken me?" (27:46). "What's happening?" the watchers whispered to each other. One ran to Him, to offer more of the drug. Others held back. "Leave him alone. Let's see if Elijah comes to save him." Ghoulishly curious, strangely uninvolved, they watched as the drama unfolded.

Then came another cry from the cross—a cry like a triumphant shout. The figure jerked—and slumped in relaxation against the brutal metal restraints. Finished with His work, Jesus had dismissed His spirit (27:45-50).

At that very moment the Temple curtain, which cut off access to the Holy of Holies, was torn in two from top to bottom. An earthquake struck, rocks were ripped apart, old tombs opened, and dead men and women stood. Stunned and awestruck, the Roman officer in charge of the execution guard blurted out, "Surely he was the Son of God!" (27:54).

At evening Pilate received a rich man who asked for the privilege of burying Jesus' body. Gently, the servant King's form was laid to rest in a tomb hewn from living rock. A great boulder was rolled to block the door—and Jesus' sorrowing followers departed (27:56-61).

Unmoved by these events just as they had been unmoved by Christ's miracles, the leaders of the Jews hurried to Pilate. They told him of Jesus' talk of rising from the dead, and urged the Roman governor to place a military guard over the tomb to keep the disciples from stealing the body. Soldiers were assigned from troops detailed to the high priest's guard. The boulder was sealed, the guard set.

And the chief priests and Pharisees retired. Triumphant? Afraid? We do not know. But surely Jesus Himself was dead. There was nothing more to do but wait.

And so, these men desperately hoped, His story had come to its tragic end.

WHY?

All Christians from the earliest days of the Church have looked to Jesus' Cross and Resurrection as the central facts of the Christian faith, through which the incarnate God reconciled us to Himself. Peter, in his first sermon, said that this Jesus was "handed over to you by God's set purpose and foreknowledge"—and loosed from death because it was "impossible for death to keep its hold on him" (Acts 2:23, 24). Only much later would this question be asked: Why was Jesus' death essential in God's "definite plan"?

Atonement theories. One of the first theories advanced saw Jesus' death as a ransom price paid to the devil, in whose kingdom mankind lived enchained. But Scripture says that Christ died not to pay but to "destroy him who holds the power of death—that is, the devil" (Heb. 2:14). Christ's death was no price paid to Satan but a battleground on which Satan met decisive defeat.

Anselm of Canterbury (11th/12th century) probed deeply to explore why God's love is expressed through atonement. *The Zondervan Pictorial Encyclopedia of the Bible* summarizes Anselm's answer expressed in *Cur Deus Homo* (Why did God become man?):

> His answer was that though prompted by His love to redeem us, God must do so in a manner consistent with His justice. The necessity of the Atonement, then, is an inference from the character of God. Sin is a revolt against God,

179

and He must inevitably react against it with wrath. Sin creates an awful liability and the inexorable demands of the divine justice must be met. The truth that God is love does not stand alone in the Bible. The God of the Bible keeps wrath for His enemies (Nah. 1:2); he is "of purer eyes than to behold evil" (Hab. 1:13, KJV). The God of Jesus is to be feared as one "who can destroy both soul and body in hell" (Mt. 10:28). "The wrath of God," wrote Paul, "is being revealed from heaven against all the godlessness and wickedness of men" (Rom. 1:18).

Therefore the death of Christ is the way in which God shows that He is righteous in forgiving sins and justifying him who has faith in Jesus (Rom. 3:24-26). God justly demands satisfaction for one's sins, and since by Christ's death, satisfaction is given, the sinner is forgiven and the punishment remitted.

Anselm's theory, of vicarious or substitutionary atonement, has dominated orthodox tradition. Christ's death is seen as *for* us, *and in our place.*

A third theory, which has characterized Protestant liberalism, is the "moral influence" theory. This also has its roots in the 11th and 12th centuries. According to this theory, Jesus' death demonstrates God's forgiving love, and stirs up a responding love in men which leads them to repent of their sins.

Scripture's testimony. Scripture itself speaks with a

clear and unmistakable voice about the death of
Christ and its meaning. It is so clear that "atonement theories" hardly seem needed; the Word is
explicit.

> In fact, the law requires that nearly everything
> be cleansed with blood, and without the shed-
> ding of blood there is no forgiveness.
>
> *Hebrews 9:22*

> This priest [Christ] . . . offered for all time one
> sacrifice for sins . . . because by one sacrifice he
> has made perfect forever those who are being
> made holy.
>
> *Hebrews 10:12, 14*

> [Jesus said,] This is my blood of the covenant,
> which is poured out for many for the forgive-
> ness of sins.
>
> *Matthew 26:28*

> God demonstrates his own love for us in this:
> While we were still sinners, Christ died for us.
> Since we have now been justified by his blood,
> how much more shall we be saved from God's
> wrath through him!
>
> *Romans 5:8, 9*

> God presented [Jesus] as a sacrifice of atone-
> ment, through faith in his blood. He did this
> to demonstrate his justice, because in his
> forbearance he had left the sins committed
> beforehand unpunished—he did it to demon-
> strate his justice at the present time, so as to be

just and the one who justifies the man who has faith in Jesus.

Romans 3:25-26

For God was pleased to have all his fulness dwell in him [Jesus], and through him to reconcile to himself all things, whether things on earth or things in heaven, by making peace through his blood, shed on the cross. . . . But now he has reconciled you by Christ's physical body through death to present you holy in his sight, without blemish and free from accusation.

Colossians 1:19-22

But now in Christ Jesus you who once were far away have been brought near through the blood of Christ. For he himself is our peace.

Ephesians 2:13, 14

He himself bore our sins in his body on the cross, so that we might die to sins and live for righteousness.

I Peter 2:24

To him who loves us and has freed us from our sins by his blood.

Revelation 1:5

He died for all that those who live should no longer live for themselves, but for him who died for them and was raised again. God . . . reconciled us to himself through Christ . . . not counting men's sins against them.

II Corinthians 5:15, 18, 19

God made him who had no sin to be sin for us, so that in him we might become the righteousness of God.

II Corinthians 5:21

Bearing the weight of our sin, in our place, Jesus shed His blood to set us free.

GOING DEEPER

to personalize

1. Study carefully Isaiah 53 (pp. 171-173). What does it tell you about the nature and results of Christ's death? From it, what would you say in answer to Anselm's question, *Cur Deus Homo?* (Why did God become man?)

2. Pages 181 and 182 quote just a few of the many verses in Scripture dealing with the reason for and results of Jesus' death. From them, write a brief statement of what Jesus' death means for you.

3. Using a concordance, look up other verses speaking of Jesus' blood and His death. See if you can summarize the teaching of the Bible on the meaning of Jesus' death in a three-page paper.

to probe

1. Compare in at least three theology texts the discussion of Jesus' atonement.

2. Three key words which speak of the meaning of Jesus' death are: reconciliation, redemption, propitiation. Find a clear definition for each.

183

ALIVE AGAIN—AND NOW

ENEMIES AND FRIENDS of Jesus waited.

On the third day after Jesus' death, two Marys went to see the tomb. They were stunned to come upon a deserted garden.

The guard the Jewish elders had posted was gone. The stone that had sealed the entrance of the tomb was rolled away. Sitting on it was an angel, whose appearance had jolted the guard to insensibility, and who now spoke to the women: "Do not be afraid, for I know that you are looking for Jesus, who was crucified. He is not here; he has risen, just as he said" (28:5, 6).

THE RESURRECTION

The Resurrection was an unexpected event. Even though the Lord had foretold His resurrection, the disciples were unprepared and found it hard to believe when the reports began to come in.

During the forty days that Jesus remained with His disciples after the Resurrection, many proofs were given. Paul reports:

> For what I received I passed on to you as of first importance: that Christ died for our sins according to the Scriptures, that he was buried, that he was raised on the third day according to the Scriptures, and that he appeared to Peter, and then to the Twelve. After that, he appeared to more than five hundred of the brothers at the same time, most of whom are still living, though some have fallen asleep. Then he appeared to James, then to all the apostles, and last of all he appeared to me also, as to one abnormally born.
>
> *I Corinthians 15:3-8*

The resurrection of Christ is one of the most thoroughly attested facts of history, not only through the written documents of the Scriptures, but also by the transformation of the disciples. From a group of men cowering in a locked room for fear of the Jews (Jn. 20:19), these men were transformed into bold and joyful witnesses of the resurrection of their Lord. The historical fact reported in Scripture, accepted by faith by believers, is a cornerstone of our faith.

Resurrection's place in the New Testament. The New Testament gives the Resurrection a central place.

186

Each of the Gospels climaxes with a description of this great act of God. The earliest preaching of the Gospel takes the Resurrection as its keynote (cf. Acts 2, 3, 4, 5, 7, 10). Paul in I Corinthians 15 argues that Christianity stands or falls with the Resurrection, the decisive turning point in mankind's history. Dying, Jesus won us forgiveness. Rising, He presents us with all the benefits of a renewed life (cf. Rom. 4:25; 5:9, 10; 8:1, 2; I Cor. 1:30).

Resurrection's nature. Christ's resurrection was the resurrection of a real body of flesh. Jesus' followers recognized His face and voice (Mt. 28:9; Lk. 24:31; Jn. 20:16, 19, 20; 21:12). His body was touched by them (Mt. 28:9; Lk. 24:39; Jn. 20:17, 27). He ate with them (Jn. 21:12, 13; Lk. 24:30, 42, 43). He Himself pointed out that "a ghost does not have flesh and bones, as you see I have" (Lk. 24:39).

Yet His resurrection body shows a unique freedom from the limitations placed on us today. He appeared among them in a locked room (Jn. 20:19), and vanished at will (Lk. 24:31). He ascended into Heaven before the disciples and many witnesses (Acts 1). Although made of flesh and bone, Jesus' resurrection body is called by Paul "spiritual"—not immaterial, but controlled by or responsive to the spirit (I Cor. 15:44). In I Corinthians 15, Paul described Christ's body as imperishable, glorious, powerful, incorruptible, immortal, and victorious.

And we are promised that our resurrection state will be like His.

MATTHEW'S EMPHASIS

Matthew 28:16-20

Each of the four Gospel writers gives extensive space to the Resurrection, and each has his own particular emphasis. Matthew's emphasis is in fullest harmony with the theme and thrust of his book. Jesus, the glorious King who lived as a servant, did establish a Kingdom. Christ's last recorded words in Matthew echo the command of the King to the servants He leaves in charge of His possessions:

> All authority in heaven and on earth has been given to me. Therefore go and make disciples of all nations, baptizing them in the name of the Father and of the Son and of the Holy Spirit, and teaching them to obey everything I have commanded you. And surely I will be with you always, to the very end of the age.
>
> *Matthew 28:18-20*

All authority. It's important to realize first of all that Jesus' Kingdom does exist today. The fact that the Old Testament visible form of the Kingdom has not yet been established in no way means that Jesus' power or authority over this earth is limited. The fact is that Jesus reigns now. His Kingdom exists alongside and within human cultures and societies, focused in the men and women in whom His Spirit dwells. His quiet, unobtrusive rule is nevertheless totally real. Nothing can happen on Heaven or on earth except by His will.

188

Just as Jesus chose during His days on earth to give men freedom to respond to or to reject Him, the pattern of our world today shows a similar freedom. When Christ returns, His righteous ways will be *imposed*. Today, He permits men to choose; most men choose the ways of sin.

But Jesus continues on the throne, and He does intervene today on our behalf as we choose to live by His will.

Make disciples. Jesus' command to us as servants, left in charge of our Lord's possessions while He is away, is very specific. When He returns and sits on His glorious throne, then Christ will impose righteousness on the whole world. Until then, the Kingdom continues as a hidden thing, revealed only to the eyes of faith, and experienced only by those who follow in the footsteps of the King.

Christ's words to the disciples here and in Matthew 16 give us direction for our lives. "If anyone would come after me," He told the twelve, "he must deny himself and take up his cross and follow me" (vs. 24). In following Jesus we find not an earthly kingdom but ourselves. We become new men and new women whose lives are being transformed and personalities reshaped to reflect the love, the compassion, and the character of the King.

Making disciples who will be like the Master (Lk. 6:40) is the calling which you and I have from our Lord and King.

All nations. The Kingdom of God in its present form cuts across all languages and boundaries and

189

societies. Men of every culture are called, not to become like those of some other nation, but to become like Jesus and reflect Him in their own land. Baptism, which speaks of identification, is to be into the Father, Son, and Holy Spirit—not into the "Western world" or into America's idea of the Church.

Thus, Christ's Kingdom is universal, and the Sermon on the Mount is a unique expression of a reality that cuts across all cultures. Unlike the coming Kingdom, which will shatter the kingdoms and the cultures of this world, the Kingdom today *infuses*. God's Kingdom today touches men, shaping within them Christ's unique concern and love for others. Individuals from every land and age respond, and, in becoming followers of the King, demonstrate the transforming power of Christ in fresh and ever-living ways.

Teaching them to observe all that I have commanded you. The disciple expresses allegiance to his King through obedience. Christ's instructions to His disciples about their own life-style are to be communicated to each new generation of believers. The Sermon on the Mount, the way of greatness, the challenge to watch and to serve while the Master is away, are all basic to the Gospel today.

In Matthew, we have been shown a way of life, amplified in the rest of the New Testament but unmistakably clear in this gospel. In Matthew's portrait of Jesus, we have a model of the men and women you and I are to be.

Jesus lived and died as a *servant* King. In the

words of this final command, "Obey everything I have commanded you," we hear echoes of His earlier words.

> It is enough for the student to be like his teacher, and the servant like his master (10:25).

> Whoever wants to become great among you must be your servant, and whoever wants to be first must be your slave—just as the Son of Man did not come to be served, but to serve, and to give his life a ransom for many" (20:26-28).

I am with you always. It's important, as we face the meaning of Christ's Kingdom and His kingship over us, to realize that we are not left alone to do the impossible. Christ has all authority, and Christ promises to be with us. What is impossible for us is fully possible for Him. We are free to follow, for we do not follow alone.

It is this reality that Paul writes of in Romans 8:11, "If the Spirit of him who raised Jesus from the dead is living in you, he who raised Christ from the dead will also give life to your mortal bodies through his Spirit, who lives in you." Christ was raised from the dead by the power of God. That same resurrection power is available to overcome the deadness in our lives. Because Christ promises to be with us always, we know that His power is always ours.

191

The King lives.
And reigns.
In us, as in all the world.

THE BREAKING

Luke 24:13-35

There is a resurrection story in Luke which helps us grasp the uniqueness of Matthew's picture of Jesus—and of the Kingdom of which you and I are a part.

On the Resurrection day, two disciples were returning to their Emmaus home, about seven miles from Jerusalem. They were talking about the events of the passion week, and the strange reports of the morning.

As they walked they were joined by a third person. He questioned them about what had been happening. As they strode along together, the two told the stranger about Jesus, who they had hoped was to be the one to redeem Israel. How amazed they were now at the report that He had been seen alive again!

Then the stranger interrupted: "How foolish you are, and how slow of heart that you do not believe all that the prophets have spoken! Did not the Christ have to suffer these things and then enter his glory?" (24:25, 26). Then He traced the Old Testament prophecies that foretold the events of that week and of His coming.

When they arrived at the village, the two urged their companion to stay for a meal and the night.

Seated, he took the bread and blessed it—and broke it. And their eyes were opened. They recognized Jesus!

There's something about the breaking of a loaf of bread. The rich odor of its goodness fills the room. The odor awakens hunger—a hunger that demands satisfaction. All this is known in the breaking of the bread.

This also is how Jesus is known. King He is. But at Passover, Jesus identified Himself as bread: "This is my body, which is broken for you" (I Cor. 11:24, KJV).

Had Jesus come in glory first, we would have known His power. But God's great love is not known in His glory, but in His brokenness. Not in His throne, but in His Cross. Not in might, but in servanthood. As the rich warm odors given off in the breaking of the bread invite men to the feast, it is in the servanthood of Jesus we are shown God's love and sense His invitation to draw near.

So it is to be with us. There is time enough for glory when Jesus comes. Today the hidden Kingdom is revealed as we, following our King, humble ourselves to serve. Humble and broken, as was our Lord in the service of His fellowmen, we best fulfill His last command.

GOING DEEPER

to personalize

1. Look at I Corinthians 15 to explore the significance of the Resurrection to our faith.

193

FIGURE VII

THEMATIC OUTLINE OF MATTHEW

Chapter	Theme	Contribution
1, 2	Birth of the King	Demonstrates that Jesus is the expected Messiah
3, 4	Baptism and temptation	Demonstrates Jesus' full identity with man—and victory over human weaknesses
5—7	Sermon on the Mount	Contains Jesus' exposition of the Kingdom life-style
8—11	Jesus' authority demonstrated	Proved Jesus' authority over what binds men (8, 9), and shows servant character of His authority (10, 11)
12—15	Growing opposition	Pinpoints opposition in Pharisaism (12, 15), and consequent modification of Kingdom's expression (13)
15—17	Kingdom's present focus	Develops contrast between expected and present form
18—20	Kingdom greatness	Examines Greatness to emphasize servanthood
21—23	Confrontation	Pronounces the King's judgment on His enemies
24—25	The future Kingdom	Gives Jesus' prophetic promise of the expected Kingdom's appearance
26—27	The King crucified	Records the execution of the King
28	Resurrection	Tells of the King raised to reign

2. Master the chart on page 194. This will enable you to think through the Book of Matthew in order to master its themes and development.

3. Study Matthew 28:18-20 (see text, pp. 188-191). What does this final command of the King in Matthew say to *you?* How are you going to obey and fulfill it?

4. What is the difference between "evangelizing" and "making disciples"? Or is there any difference?

to probe

1. Select any chapter of the Book of Matthew and, using the chart on page 194 as an aid, demonstrate how that chapter fits the theme and emphasis of the book.

2. Quickly read through either Mark or Luke. How does the development of this book differ from that of Matthew? Can you catch a glimpse of the purpose of the book you just read? What seems to you to be its major thrust or emphasis?

3. The Gospels are an introduction to the New Testament, not an end to the story of Jesus. To trace what happens next as the body of believers begins to take form and develop its own way of life, read the next book in this **Bible Alive Series:** *The Great Adventure.*